Meeting the Needs of Children

Creating Trust and Security

Louis E. Raths

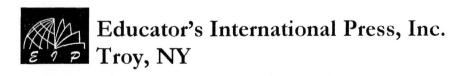

Educator's International Press, Inc.
Troy, NY

Raths, Louis E.

Published by Educator's International Press, Inc.
18 Colleen Road
Troy, N. Y. 12180

Previously published by Charles Merrill Publishing Co. © Louis E. Raths 1972 (previous ISBN 0-675-09130-6)

Library of Congress Catalog Card Number: 98-70460

ISBN   0-9658339-7-6

Manufactured in the United States of America

03 02 01 00 99 98   1 2 3 4 5 6

Preface to the 1998 Edition

Louis E. Raths (1900 - 1978) is perhaps best remembered for the book, *Values and Teaching*, which advanced the controversial theory of "values clarification." The republication of this lesser known volume, *Meeting the Needs of Children: Creating Trust and Security*, is a timely event. In the last half century, divorce rates have climbed, blended families appear to be the norm, and far too many children find their only source of stability and trust in their schooling. In both suburban and urban settings, most teachers can readily provide accounts of children living in circumstances that seem unconscionable. This volume provides a theoretical framework and suggestions for concrete interventions that teachers might try in their own classrooms to help children who may have unmet emotional needs which interfere with academic achievement. What is most valuable about this book is that Raths reminds us that at the heart of all education is the need for children to be treated with dignity and respect and that meeting the emotional needs of children is a fundamental aspect of the teacher's role.

Louis Raths received his doctorate from Ohio State University in 1933 under the direction of Ralph Tyler. After working as a school administrator for two years, Raths returned to Columbus to join the evaluation staff of the Eight-year Study, headed by Tyler. As a member of the Ohio State faculty from the mid-1930s until 1947, Raths served with scholars such as Boyd H. Bode, H. Gordon Hullfish, Hilda Taba, Alan F. Griffin, and Carl Rogers. Like many of his colleagues who were also influenced by progressive education, Raths developed a career-long interest in reflective thinking, valuing, and the emotional needs of children.

While at Ohio State, Raths developed the theoretical approach which characterized his three major works, *Values and Teaching* (1966, 1978), *Teaching for Thinking* (1967, 1986), and *Meeting the Needs of Children* (1972). The thesis advanced in each work evolved from Raths' work with a group of physicians at Ohio State on the problem of defining the concept "health." Raths learned that little consensus could be reached among the physicians until the discussion turned to defining "illness." In the field of education, Raths reasoned, it may by more productive to focus on symptoms of what might be termed "educational illnesses" and their treatment rather than trying to reach consensus on the problem of defining educational aims in an affirmative manner.

Thus, each of these three works shares this common method: behavioral "symptoms" are associated with a difficulty in the area of values, thinking, or needs. For example, in *Values and Teaching*, overconformity is posited as an indicator of a problem with the process of valuing. Then, curricular interventions are prescribed that invite the child to engage in experiences that address the area of difficulty. Raths and his coauthors, Merrill Harmin and Sidney B. Simon, suggested that teachers should provide the overconforming child with ample opportunities to engage in valuing in the curriculum. The hypothesis was that the symptoms would wane as the child gained more experience in the area of hypothesized weakness.

In *Meeting the Needs of Children*, which first partially appeared in booklet form developed with Professor Anna Burrell in the 1950s, Raths posited a connection between unmet emotional needs and five types of problematic behaviors: aggression, submission, social withdrawal, regression, and the manifestation of psychosomatic symptoms. In other words, when a child consistently displays a pattern of behavior that is characterized by one or more of these symptoms, then the child may be experiencing an unmet emotional need. Using the medical analogy again, Raths pointed out that it is inappropriate to punish the aggressive child for his or her behavior— certainly the most common approach in trying to control aggression. As he pointed out, while control is sometimes necessary for safety's sake, what is needed is an effort to understand and treat the causes of such behavior. He wrote, "We punish the child for his aggressiveness rather than making an attempt to understand and treat the causes. We would not say of the sixteen-year-old child who had a temperature of 103 degrees that . . . he is too old to have a temperature." (p. 24).

In this way, as in *Values and Teaching* and *Teaching for Thinking*, Raths expressed an impatience with the traditional treatment for common educational problems.   In *Values and Teaching*, he noted that indoctrination and imposition have generally been an ineffective route to the development of values.   In *Teaching for Thinking*, he argued that children have been told again and again to not be so impulsive—to stop and think.   Here again is an effort to get at the deeper source of the problem and intervene in a more effective manner.   The question this book attempts to address is how can teachers help children who are exhibiting the five behavioral symptoms associated with unmet needs, not how to more efficiently control the children.

For all the rhetoric about symptoms and diagnosis, it is important to remember that the analogy from medicine is only an analogy.   Raths did not advocate the literal application of the medical model in education, as is currently the practice in special education.   Raths argued that if a teacher believed a child had an unmet need, then it was a signal to the teacher to manipulate the classroom environment in such a way that there would be a greater chance for the need to be met.   The focus here is on the interaction between the child and his/her environment, without the attribution of a trait or disorder.   After all, we all have emotional needs.   The medical model as it has been adopted in special education does not tend to take this interactionist perspective, but rather identifies some trait located in the child—a learning disability, a behavior disorder, and so on—that requires treatment.

While Raths posited eight emotional needs for study, he did not focus heavily on their source or the complex interaction of personality and social structure that results in different outcomes for individuals under similar circumstances.   He wrote that needs are not innate, but socially conditioned.   While curious about the source of needs, the search for their ultimate source seemed to open a hopelessly difficult problem, one characterized by infinite regress.   He chose to center on the more proximate problem of the linkage between emotional needs and behavior.   The research conducted on the "needs theory" largely supported the hypothesis advanced in the text.

Some contemporary educational theorists would no doubt find fault with this research for not going deeper into the nature of needs themselves and the structural mechanisms in our society which frustrate the meeting of emotional needs.   It would be a mistake, however, to see this work as apolitical or divorced from larger social concerns. Raths made it clear that not only is academic achievement and individual well-being threatened by the manifestation of these "symptomatic behaviors," but democracy is weakened as well. Democracy, in the Deweyan sense, cannot thrive where individuals are persistently aggressive, submissive, socially isolated, developmentally regressive, or suffer from psychosomatic illnesses. These behaviors interfere with the process of purposing, of planning reflectively and collectively. *Meeting the Needs of Children* suggests to the classroom teacher some insightful ways in which children who suffer from these behaviors can be helped.

Although Raths contributed the major theoretical effort in each of his works, much credit for the publication of these fine books must go to his coauthors. Selma Wassermann, Arnold Rothstein, and Arthur Jonas—all doctoral students at NYU who studied with Raths—devoted their dissertation research to testing various aspects of these theories and contributed greatly to the publication of the first edition of *Teaching for Thinking* (1967). They were also responsible for the publication of the second edition in 1986. Wassermann has continued to advance the field of teacher education and curriculum with the publication of a number of important works, including her two most recent volumes on case method in teacher education.   Sidney B. Simon and Merrill Harmin similarly contributed to the development of *Values and Teaching* and continued to work in the area of affective education. Anna Burrell's work on the needs theory was invaluable.

Individuals who want to learn more about Louis Raths' work would benefit from reading the "classic" works themselves, and then turning to some of the best of the secondary sources. Because much of what has been written about values clarification is erroneous or relies on other secondary sources, careful readers really need to examine the primary sources for themselves. One excellent secondary source stands out: James Beane's volume, *Affect in the Curriculum: Toward Democracy, Dignity, and Diversity*, which offers an accurate and thoughtful account of values clarification.

On a personal note, as Louis Raths' granddaughter, it is very gratifying to see this work republished. My family is indebted to Sarah Biondello of Educator's International Press for her interest, guidance, and hard work in pursuing this project. These published works constitute an important part of Louis Raths' contribution to curriculum theory and teacher education. For my father, an educational researcher and teacher educator, and I—and many of his colleagues and graduate students—Louis Raths' influence is more deeply manifested in the dispositions and habits of mind he cultivated. He taught us to "prize doubt" as the starting point of all inquiry, to seek alternatives and examine their consequences, and finally, encouraged us to choose well.

While both the publisher and I are quite well aware of changes in style and language as well as advances in the literature over the last twenty-six years, we have chosen to reissue this classic text exactly as it was first published with only the addition of this preface. Of course, were we to re-edit the text, we would change the exclusive use of male pronouns, change Negro to Black or African American, and possibly update some of the scenarios. However, we feel that these are artifacts of the time, place, and circumstances under which the book was written. The heart of the book lies in its intrinsic notions of the emotional needs of children and the value placed upon the knowledge and efforts of teachers to enable children to overcome emotional deficit and neglect. Our goal was to preserve the integrity of Raths' original writing and thoughts while placing this fine work in the context of the 1990s.

Amy McAninch,
Assistant Professor, Saint Mary College
Leavenworth, Kansas
February, 1998

References

Beane, James A. *Affect in the Curriculum: Toward Democracy, Dignity, and Diversity*. New York: Teachers College Press, 1990.

Raths, Louis E. *An Application to Education of the Needs Theory*. Bronxville, NY: Modern Educational Services, 1949.

Raths, Louis E.; & Burrell, Anna P. *Do's & Dont's of the Needs Theory*. Bronxville, NY: Modern Educational Services, 1951.

Raths, Louis E.; & Burrell, Anna P. *Understanding the Problem Child*. West Orange, NJ: The Economics Press, 1963.

Raths, Louis E.; Harmin, Merrill; & Simon, Sidney B. *Values and Teaching*. Columbus, OH: Charles Merrill, 1978, 1966.

Raths, Louis E.; Wassermann, Selma; Jonas, Arthur; & Rothstein, Arnold M. *Teaching for Thinking: Theory, Strategies, and Activities for the Classroom*. New York: Teachers College Press, 1986.

Wassermann, Selma *Introduction to Case Method Teaching: A Guide to the Galaxy*. New York: Teachers College Press, 1994.

Wassermann, Selma *Serious Players in the Primary Classroom: Empowering the Young Child Through Active Learning Experiences*. New York: Teachers College Press, 1990

PREFACE

Suppose, for the moment, that you are a teacher, and that you have in your classroom a boy who is very aggressive. Let us further suppose that you have decided that one very important cause of his aggressiveness is a lack of love and affection in his life; that is to say: he *needs* love and affection. Let us assume that you try every day in every way that you can think of to bring more warmth, more love, more affection into his life. You do this over and over again and you do it for many weeks. You see changes in the boy, great changes. In terms both of frequency and of intensity, his aggression declines markedly. He seems to be a very different person. What have you proved by this series of operations?

Have you proved that he had a need for love and affection? Hardly. You assumed that he did, and having assumed it, you tried to bring love and affection to him.

Have you proved that you did, at least partially, *meet* his need for love and affection? There really is no *proof* that you *met* his need. It is true, of course, that he had been very aggressive, and when you treated him consistently with love and warmth and affection, he became a different person. His aggression declined greatly. But that does not constitute *proof* that you really and truly met *a need that he had* for love and affection.

What then can we say about all your labors in behalf of this one child? What did you prove, or what can we say you established by doing what you did? The answer is a rather long and involved one: you can say that you made certain assumptions about his needs, and when you worked with him *in the ways that you did,* his behavior changed markedly. In this volume, various ways of working with aggressive children are spelled out in great detail. No teacher would use all of them, and no teacher would use only those that are cited in this book. Practically every teacher creates another or several other ways as she *tries to meet* the needs of children.

Sometime during the early years of the Second World War, I had been formulating an extension of the frustration-aggression hypothesis. It seemed to me that extreme submission was also a probable consequence of frustration, and I came to believe that children who tended to withdraw from the company of others might also be suffering from frustration. Probably because of my work with the Eight Year Study and my contacts with Carolyn Zachry, Alice Keliher, Lawrence Frank, Daniel Prescott, and others, I became convinced that we should take a greater interest in the mental health of children, and that we should do more about "meeting the needs of children."

At that time I was spending one, sometimes two, and often three days each week with classroom teachers in the public schools of Ohio. I seized these opportunities to talk about some of the probable emotional needs of children. Many of those teachers were extremely helpful to me at the time. They were patient with me. They made studies of individual children, and in small group meetings we exchanged ideas about hypothetical needs. We began to think about practical ways of *trying* to meet the needs we assumed to be present.

Out of these labors I formulated a list of eight needs, eight so-called emotional needs, that seem to be indoctrinated into our children by the child-rearing processes of our culture. With the fashioning of this. list, we were now ready to carry out some doctoral researches in the field. Anna Carol Fults, a graduate student at Ohio State University, carried out a doctoral study in a junior high school in Arkansas. She operated a program that is outlined in the present volume. First, she had teachers identify children who were unusually aggressive, or unusually submissive, or unusually withdrawn in their behavior. Second, along with the teachers, she studied the behavior of these children to see if there were any clues that would indicate that one or more of the eight emotional needs were *not* being met. Third, she helped the teachers to discover and apply ways that seemed to be of help in efforts to meet the needs which had been identified. Fourth, she tried to get evidence of change or lack of change in the behavior of the children.

Her experiment or study was spectacularly successful. In fact, it was almost too good to be true. I became convinced that it was some unique qualities possessed by Anna Carol Fults, or some unique qualities possessed by these Arkansas teachers, or a combination of both that was really responsible for the changes in the students. It was hard to believe that consistent, focused attention to the assumed needs of these children could have so profound an influence upon the behavior of children. Even so and not withstanding, we began to formulate a list of dos and don'ts for other teachers who might be interested in such a project. And here again, many public school teachers in Ohio made suggestions for additions and subtractions from this list, which was then mimeographed for distribution to many teachers in the state.

Dr. Fults completed her study in 1946, and in that year and the following year, Kathryn Feyerison carried out a similar study in an elementary school in Des Moines, Iowa. Her study, too, was characterized by significant changes in the behavior of the experimental students.

In 1947 I accepted a position in the School of Education at New York University. Very shortly thereafter I met Anna Porter Burrell, who was a doctoral student at the time. We worked together with some teachers in a public school in the Navy Yard District of Brooklyn. Mrs. Burrell made use of the experiences reported by Fults and Feyerison, and she and I spent much time together adding to the entries on the mimeographed list of the dos and don'ts of the so-called needs theory, as it came to be known at the time. Her work was also very successful, and the classroom teachers were much impressed by these ways of working with children who were normal in nearly all ways, but troublesome in others.

In 1949 Robert Fleming completed his testing of the needs theory by making a study of the relationships between symptoms of psychosomatic illness and the assumed needs of the children who were so diagnosed. In his investigation, only the family physician was allowed to make the judgment that a child's complaints were of the kind termed psychosomatic. Fleming had an experimental population that he divided into three subgroups. One group received only the kind of attention to which they were accustomed. In another grouping, both parents and teachers were counseled in relating themselves to children in ways consistent with the needs theory as it is described in the present volume. A third group was made up of children whose parents did not participate, but whose teachers did. The greatest gains were made when both teachers and parents made efforts to meet the needs of the children. Some gains were made when only the teachers made unusual efforts to meet the emotional needs of the experimental children, and little or no gain was made where the needs theory was not applied.

At about this same time, Frank Trager, an executive in the Bureau for Intercultural Education, secured the cooperation of Yale University in a needs project to be carried out with a number of Connecticut public schools. Stephen Abrahamson was in direct charge of the work, and more than one hundred teachers became involved in the study. About ninety percent of the experimental children made significant changes in their behavior. This particular study was never published, but it was presented in written form to the Bureau.

Another NYU doctoral student, Charity Mance, wanted to try the theory with populations of Negro children. She was very much interested in two questions: (1) Would Negro children show a pattern of emotional needs distinctly different from white children? (2) Would a group of experimental children do much better on thinking-type tests if their teachers put an emphasis upon meeting these eight emotional needs? Negro children showed the highest need in the area of understanding one's self in relation to society, and this was the very first time that this particular need ranked as the highest. With the other populations studied there were outstanding needs for love, for achievement, for freedom from intense feelings of fear and guilt, and for self-respect. As for the second question, the children made significantly higher scores on the tests after the experimental treatment.

In 1952 Irving Amdur completed his dissertation research on the needs theory. He applied the ideas to Puerto Rican children in a New York City public elementary school whose teachers characterized their behavior as "withdrawing." The late Dr. Amdur carried out an intensive in-service training program on the needs theory with his staff of teachers. Here again the gains made by the experimental populations were very significant. After a semester of emphasis by the teachers, it was found that the isolates and "fringers" were participating. Many of the parents of these children came to the classrooms and remarked on the changes in the behavior of their children and of their new interests in school and their new interests in other children.

A few years later (1957) Grace Ellen Stiles tested the theory by applying test procedures to samples of children with accident-repeating tendencies and to children who were not accident repeaters. She concluded that the unmet emotional needs of accident-repeating children are very significantly greater than the unmet emotional needs of accident-free children. Her research also culminated in a doctoral dissertation at New York University.

As a part of their dissertation inquiries, three young men who were teaching in a Scarsdale, N.Y., elementary school decided to include at least one needs case among their experimental children. The investigators, Arthur Jonas, Donald Martin, and Ernest Machnits, completed their work in 1960. In all three cases the results were generally favorable, and the children in their experiment made significant gains in the standardized tests which were employed by the Scarsdale system.

During the past two years Professor Rajpal, at State University College at Fredonia, N.Y., has carried on a test of the needs theory that was very different in design. In his investigation, classroom teachers identified children as aggressive, submissive, withdrawn, regressive, or *probably* suffering from psychosomatic complaints, but they did nothing special about the children so identified. Rajpal trained a group of seniors in the Department of Education in many aspects of the needs theory, and these students were made responsible for meeting with one child (the same child) every day, for one school period, over the period of one semester. Before and after ratings were made by the classroom teachers, and they were of the opinion that very significant changes in behavior had occurred in the great majority of cases. Rajpal's research report will appear in a professional journal in the near future.

In this preface I have detailed the history of some serious and penetrating investigations relating to the emotional needs of children. I thought a brief summary of the researches should be included in this extensive treatment of the theory as it applies to creating feelings of trust and security in our classrooms. While it is true that the results tend to point in a direction favorable to the theory, there were disconcerting exceptions. In more than ten percent of the total number of cases the results were *not* significant. There were some children who did not respond by changing their behavior. Whatever it was, their usual behavior persisted. I am told that I should be very happy with a proposed program that tends to succeed with much more than eighty percent of those who seem to need special attention. Even so, I continue to be plagued by the question: Why didn't it succeed with this relatively small percentage of children?

Was it incorrect diagnosis? Is it likely that these children had much deeper psychological or physical health problems and that we did not recognize them? Is it possible that the teachers did not make the kind of contact with these few children that is necessary in applying the needs theory? I hesitate to go on with other possible alternatives because I seem to hear some one say, "Sure, when it agrees with the theory, you accept it gladly; but when it does not support the theory, you blame it on something else." I must accept the facts of the situation: thus far it has worked very well with substantially more than eighty percent of the cases.

Even so, the designs of the researches leave much to be desired, and the instruments we used for measurements of change were the best we have, but that's not very good. All in all, what do these researches really prove? They support the general idea that if the ways of working with children described in this volume are carried out, a large number of children will change their behavior in ways that are more conducive to mental health and to improved learning.

In this first printing of the materials I want to thank all of those teachers who have helped in the formulation of the program, and I want to thank especially those who carried on the research in the field, those whose names have been mentioned in this preface. In the volume itself there are few references to any others because I have been concerned with the research that had direct bearing on the theory as it is here presented. I hope the materials will come to have widespread use, not only in our own country, but the world over. Love and trust and feelings of security are greatly needed today, and they will be needed in all of the tomorrows.

L. E. R.

Hickoryhurst,
Dunkirk, N.Y.

CONTENTS

To

PROFESSOR ANNA PORTER BURRELL

A friend of long standing, a colleague, and a former student who has contributed significantly to this volume. Much of her life has been devoted to advancing the emotional security of children the world over. I dedicate this shared work to her with love and respect.

The transformation of hate and aggressiveness into kindness, of destructiveness into life-furthering activities, depends upon our discovering the formative principle that prevails during the period of growth and development. . . . So the withdrawal of love and the rise of aggression go hand in hand; for love is a capacity for embracing otherness, for widening the circle of interests in which the self may operate, for begetting new forms of life.

Lewis Mumford
The Conduct of Life

I

INTRODUCTION

This book is one of several attempting to answer the following questions:

In the schoolrooms of the world, and in the homes of the world, what can teachers and parents do which would most likely contribute significantly to the fulfillment of life? What contributes most to that inward calm which we frequently call a sense of well-being? What can we do that will add to the probability that this generation of children will be more zestful, more spontaneous, more cooperative, more thoughtful and considerate of others, more ardent guardians and champions of freedom for everyone everywhere?

What can we do now that will make it more likely that these children will use their energies, their intelligence, their values, to reduce the threats of war? to conquer the blight and the sores of poverty? to carry on the fight against disease? to use what powers they have to reduce the tyranny and caprice of the powerful? to seek and to prize beauty and knowledge for their own sakes? to plan the intelligent use of the earth's resources which make life possible and fruitful?

What can we do now that will enable this generation of children to have greater control over themselves? As the result, in part, of *our*

2

efforts, will they be more likely to come to terms with their own impulses, their own inner torments and griefs? Will they expect too much of themselves and of their peers? Will they want what they cannot have, and will they reject that which is most good for man, individually and collectively?

These questions are tremendously difficult. But difficult as they may be, we have to face them. After all, we are *now* spending our time, our energies, our hopes and fears presumably toward some good ends. Whatever we are now doing, or whatever we may choose to do, will probably have some influence on the ways our children will address themselves to these problems. What then will we choose to do? Where, as teachers and parents, will we put the emphasis in our teaching and guiding?

I and other authors mentioned in connection with these issues have taken a position on this question. We believe that, first of all, we should do everything we can for the physical health of our children and their parents. Healthy children are more free to learn and to grow, more free to look inward, more free to look at alternatives, and more free to choose from them. Our great country is losing ground to other nations in nurturing the health of its people. We seem to be afraid of some bug-a-boo called "socialized medicine." Since the healthy people tend to survive, and their genes tend to be perpetuated, and since we all prize good health and recognize how important it is, we must intensify our efforts to promote the health of children, to prevent ill health, and to remedy defects as soon as possible, with all the resources available.

Good health depends upon an adequate diet, upon rest and recreation, upon decent housing, upon protection for children not yet mature enough to take full responsibility for the preservation of life and limbs. Good health includes the care of eyes and ears and teeth. Good health is so very important that we suggest that a thorough physical examination should be the starting point of any inquiry into the causes for difficulties in learning. *Step one, then, is health, physical health.*

We are all agreed, too, on the second point. We believe that emotional security is a vital constituent of a sense of well-being. When, within ourselves, we feel relatively secure, again we are more free to consult alternatives, and we are more free to choose among them. We do not believe, for example, that the whole world is in a conspiracy against us. We have some sense of self-respect, and we are reasonably free from deep feelings of fear and guilt. We have a sense of belonging and of participating in the joys and the work of the world with our peers. We have experienced a growth in our skills and competencies, we are making some sense out of the world around us, and we are confident that the social conditions are not anarchic and that we can be reasonably sure of economic security. There is an inward sense of well-being when we are emotionally secure: Our emotional needs are being fairly well met.

The present volume focuses upon this matter of some emotional needs of children (of all of us, as a matter of fact). A theory is presented which suggests that there is a close relationship between certain kinds of child behavior and unmet emotional needs. It is postulated that persistent and hostile *aggression* toward people and toward property may indeed be a visible symbol of one or more unmet emotional needs. If we work with such an aggressive child in a way which is more likely to meet his emotional needs, will he modify his behavior? There is a great deal of research evidence in support of the inference that he will indeed change.

In addition to persistent and extreme forms of aggression, there are other child (and adult) behaviors which suggest that some emotional needs are not being met. *Self-isolation,* withdrawing, running away from people, a disinclination to be with people, always being the observer and never the participant, playing the role of wallflower or fringer are possible indications of one or more unmet emotional needs.

Third, *regressions* to an earlier stage of development are often associated with emotional insecurity. The child of four or five who returns to sucking his thumb, who begins to lose control of his toilet habits, who begins to use "baby talk" again, who, in other words, wants to be an infant again, is thought to be a child with one or more unmet emotional needs.

Fourth, extreme manifestations of *submissiveness* are often taken as signs of unsatisfied emotional needs. The child seems to have no backbone. He is a captive of those around him. He seems to be afraid to dissent or to indicate what he would prefer. He often "toadies." Not infrequently this is accompanied by whimpering and crying. A sturdy *self* does not seem to be there, and one reasonable hypothesis suggests that such a child is emotionally insecure.

Fifth, and last in this listing, are symptoms of *psychosomatic illness.* In these instances the teacher or the parent does NOT make the diagnosis, but rather the family physician. At school a child with psychosomatic symptoms is apt to have an aggravation of symptoms at particular times of the day. A child may have a severe headache which manifests itself whenever there is a reading period, or a math or science period, or when it is time to go out to play. This recurrence of a physical health complaint at regular times suggests a connection between the two events and raises a question about emotional security in the particular situation. If asthma attacks come at particular times, if skin acnes become more bothersome, if stomachs begin to ache, or if bowels or bladder make insistent demands at particular periods, it may be appropriate to hypothesize a psychosomatic disturbance. This should, of course, be checked with the parents. One or more emotional needs may be unmet, and a thoughtful, compassionate teacher may do a great deal to alleviate the condition.

In all five of these extreme forms of behavior, an observer close to the child notices tension and strain, an absence of that internal sense of well-being. Moreover, all of these kinds of behavior seem to interfere with learning. The child continues to act upon his impulses with little rationality. He doesn't seem to have come to terms with himself and his own needs; he is unlikely to be poised enough to look at alternatives and to choose from them. There is a revealing of behavior that seems immature.

Suppose that we call these five behavior-pictures *gross behaviors.* Suppose, also, that we accept the proposition that these gross behaviors indicate that one or more emotional needs are not being met. What then? In this book there are many suggestions for trying to determine just which emotional needs require attention, and another section of the book concentrates its attention on things to do and things to avoid doing if you want to help meet the emotional needs of the youngster.

Earlier in this section I indicated that we placed highest priority on the physical health of children, and that if we want to help children who are having difficulty in maturing, our very first step should involve an inquiry into the health status of these boys and girls.

The second step should be a cautious and careful investigation of a child's emotional security. The present volume details ways of carrying forward such an inquiry, and many suggestions are offered about ways of working with children who seem to have unmet emotional needs.

We have asked the question: Where, as teachers and parents, will we put the emphasis in our teaching and guiding? On physical health and upon emotional security as starting places. We should also put a great emphasis upon thinking activities. In another volume dealing with these topics[1] we presented an educational theory which related

---

[1] Louis E. Raths, Selma Wassermann, Arthur Jonas, and Arnold M. Rothstein, *Teaching for Thinking, Theory and Application* (Columbus, Ohio: Charles E. Merrill Publishing Co., 1967).

behavior to the presence or absence of thinking. There we indicated that when children are overly impetuous and rash, when they are overly dependent upon those around them for help in thinking, when they are dogmatic and "loudmouthed," when they are rigid and compulsive in the presence of situations involving alternatives, when they are almost *afraid* to think, and when they assert that they don't want to think, we can be reasonably sure that they have not been exposed to a curriculum that emphasized thinking.

In that same volume fifteen different thinking operations were set forth and literally hundreds of examples given to illustrate ways by which parents and teachers could put an emphasis upon thinking as they live and work with children. Research studies were cited indicating that children do modify even their characteristic behavior when they have intensive and extensive experience with situations which require thinking.

Thinking involves a consideration of alternatives; it includes the idea of "prizing the doubt"; on many occasions it requires a search for assumptions; it often involves all of our senses; it sometimes results in the formulation of tentative hypotheses; it includes the ideas of classifying and interpreting, and many more. On some occasions it calls for a questioning of authorities. Many, many times it involves criticism. Along with all of these there are problem solving and decision making and a host of others. Confronted daily with activities which require thought, which often require suspended judgment, which almost always require some qualifying of the conclusions, children are learning habits which tend to contribute to inner peace, to a sense of well-being. They are becoming problem or thinking oriented and will have less of a tendency to panic or be depressed when confronted with ambiguous, doubtful, or problematic situations.

The fourth center of emphasis recommended by the authors referred to has to do with the development of values. Although we place physical health first, emotional security second, and thinking activities third on the list, we do believe that the clarification and development of values should be a most important concern of parents and teachers. One entire volume has been devoted to this topic.[2] We believe that it is much more difficult for today's children to develop values, and we indicate many reasons for this in the volume. We have there taken the position that certain trends in the behavior of a child indicate a need for an emphasis upon values in his educa-

---

[2] Louis E. Raths, Merrill Harmin, and Sidney B. Simon, *Values and Teaching* (Columbus, Ohio: Charles E. Merrill Publishing Co., 1966).

tion. Where children are extremely apathetic, or where they are extremely flighty, or where they are characteristically over-conforming or over-dissenting, where they are extremely uncertain and unable to choose among alternatives, where they seem to swing from one extreme to the other, where they pretend a great deal and assume a variety of roles, and where they consistently under-achieve, we accept these behaviors as symptomatic of a lack of value development. Notice how these behaviors bear upon an inward sense of well-being. If values give direction to life, if values make a difference, if values reflect a sense of purpose, of something prized and cherished, the absence of values would suggest a lack of zestful living, a life with little fulfillment.

The volume *Values and Teaching* presents many ideas for teachers and parents to use with children if an emphasis is to be put upon the clarifying and development of values. Thus far, then, the associated authors of these volumes recommend an emphasis upon physical health, emotional security, thinking activities, and the clarification and development of values. Are there more?

Yes, and included among them one very important emphasis is needed, we believe. We refer to the development of status among one's peers and the development of high morale in groups that work together. While power may tend to corrupt, and absolute power may corrupt absolutely, the absence of power also corrupts. Where there is no power, the people perish. John Stuart Mill once said, "A state which dwarfs its men . . . will find that with small men no great thing can really be accomplished." A state that shortchanges its people in the field of physical health, a state which is indifferent to the emotional needs of its children, a state that restricts the free exchange of ideas and discourages thinking, a state that puts little emphasis upon the clarifying of values, a state that is forgetful of the need we all have to feel some sense of power is indeed dwarfing us all, and under those circumstances we cannot look forward to the accomplishment of great things.

A forthcoming volume deals with the relationship of power and morale and its place in the training of teachers. It is a necessary ingredient of a wholesome feeling of security.

Can we join together in a united effort to emphasize these five things in our schools and in our homes, and can we then look forward to a better, a fuller, a more zestful life for all of us and our children?

2

EARLY CHILDHOOD
AND
THE NEEDS THEORY

.Before we talk about responsibilities of teachers in meeting the emotional needs of children, we ought to turn back and see how some of these needs come into existence. We need to know something about child growth and development in the very early days of life.

We know that the arrival of the new baby heralds a day of happiness in most homes. The relationship between mother and child is one of tremendous warmth and affection. The new infant is kissed and caressed; he is hugged and petted and fondled; he is made much of. The mother smiles at the child, sings to him. The environment is hushed when he sleeps. The mother is gentle in her handling of the infant, and almost every touch is intended as a caress. This warm and friendly atmosphere is probably generated in part by the inability of the baby to do anything for himself—he is so helpless, so dependent, and so much a part of the mother's life. This helplessness seems to call forth an abundance of protection, of sheltering, of love and affection. When all goes well in the family, the mother and child work out a relationship of trust that brings inner security to both of them. The child comes to depend upon the mother for many services. His reactions call forth responses from the mother, just as the mother's reactions elicit responses from her baby. They live together in this very warm emotional climate; as the baby begins to have a deep and abiding faith in the relationship, his inner security is strengthened day by day. He comes to feel that people are good, that they can be trusted, and that he can be confident in his relationships with them that the trust will continue. This picture of the early months of life is true—*if it is true!* In other words, there are mother-child relationships that do not produce this inner security, this faith, this deep and abiding trust. The relationships are unstable and unpredictable and contribute to distrust, uncertainty and doubt. The question before us is to suggest what happens to personalities that are insecure in their early childhood. Lewis Mumford has indicated the importance of the loving trusting relationships in such a commonplace activity as eating:

> "So, too, the infant who is offered food without friendly intercourse and love, as in an old-fashioned orphanage, may reject it or fail to be nourished by an otherwise adequate diet; the very processes of digestion prosper only if reinforced by attitudes and feelings that have no direct bearing on the function in hand."[1]

It would not be accurate to say that these early days and these early months settle the problem of inner security for all time to come. Parents and infants who establish this wonderfully loving, trustful relationship are going to experience situations in the future that will threaten the growing child. Absences from home on the part of daddy, who might have to go to war or who might have to go away on another job, long illnesses on the part of mother, or separation or divorce of parents, or even death of the mother might threaten deeply the security that was once established. In later years the coming of a new baby might present a similar threat. Unusual situations in life itself, in the schoolroom or a new social class setting, might provoke distrust and rejection and increase insecurity. In fact, during one's whole life this problem of increased trust in human relations, of increased inner security, is one that must be faced as one meets life's situations. A person with a good start has a better chance of meeting the challenge than a person with a poor beginning. On the other hand, a person with a good start may meet situations that challenge security and may lose much of it in certain crucial situations. We shall speak again later of some of the consequences of frustration.

---

[1] Lewis Mumford, *The Conduct of Life* (New York: Harcourt Brace & Co., 1951), p. 126.

Before many months have passed, the new baby begins to do things, and these are great days for the parents. The first smile, the first solid food that is eaten, the first steps that are taken, the first intelligible sounds that are made are taken as occasions for lavishing praise on the child. In fact, beginning at about eight or nine months of age, a good share of the child's waking moments are spent in receiving some kind of recognition for what he is doing.

The child begins to experience conscious control of himself. He sees that certain things receive recognition and that many of these things are praised. He repeats and repeats those activities that seem to call forth praise and reward. He begins to feel a sense of achievement and of accomplishment. He senses himself as an independent person who has purposes and who can influence the environment around him. He is becoming a person, and a person of worth. He is esteemed by his mother and father. He is praised by them, encouraged by them, and under this system of rewards, and penalties too, he begins to take on a personality of his own.

Here again, this is not always true under the surface! Some very young infants grow up in an atmosphere where this recognition and reward and encouragement to be people in their own right, to strive and to achieve, is met alternately by parental neglect, parental disapproval, and parental penalties. Under one set of circumstances the child feels a sense of achievement; under another he feels unsure of himself, doubtful, uncertain, and feelings of achievement are thwarted or frustrated.

The children who do get a good start in life because of a healthy relationship with their parents need to have these feelings reinforced as they mature. All of us, as we grow up, do meet situations of failure or discouragement, of despair at times; and if these experiences are unusually severe or unusually prolonged or repetitive, we are apt to lose the feeling of self-respect, of personal worth, of satisfaction with the expenditure of our efforts. The probable consequences of this frustration and thwarting have already been mentioned briefly.

So far in this discussion great emphasis has been placed upon a relationship between mother and child that is characterized by love and affection and feelings of accomplishment, recognition and personal worth. These early months may also provide the growing infant with a feeling of economic security: an ample supply of food, adequate clothing and shelter. In most situations there is a stability in the living relationships over this period of time. Probably because the young child is unable to communicate his own reactions and has no standards about economic security, there is a tendency to learn that his own environment, whatever it is, is one that can be relied upon, one that can be trusted to continue. Given a reasonable certainty of supply of the basic essentials of life, this standard becomes an acceptable one, and, quite obviously, the standard varies widely among different families. The point being made here is that the growing child learns to feel this sense of economic security as much as he learns to feel a sense of achievement, and as much as he learns to feel a sense of loving trustfulness in his human relations. The actual specifications of the standard are not important; what is essential is that the child feels that his way of life will probably continue. Thus he will be given another solid start in the whole complex of things that we call "inner security." With the passing of months and years, this possible complex situation must continue to be relatively secure. Where it is threatened, where there are grave doubts and anxieties about economic security, the personality is threatened; and if a child's need for economic security is thwarted, we may again anticipate what the consequences will be, but this discussion will be postponed until later.

We have said that a child *learns* to need love and affection as he tries to establish relationships with his mother. We have said that the growing child *learns* to need recognition, praise, and reward in his relationships to his parents. We have said that a child *learns* to need a feeling of economic security in his life. There is some evidence that the infant child may bring some of these needs into the world with him, that they are in part inherited, and in part influenced by prenatal experiences. In this present report, however, emphasis is given to the part that culture plays in instigating needs. It is here believed that children are indoctrinated by the culture (parents and others) with the need for love and affection, praise, and economic security among others. For the most part, these needs are *learned* by the child. As he lives he comes to have them as needs, and then, if they are thwarted or frustrated, behavior is seriously influenced.

In the early months and years of a child's life, another emotional need seems to be indoctrinated. As a member of the family he comes to have the feeling that he "belongs," and as he grows older this feeling of belongingness to a family is emphasized. Still later, through the interaction of his parents, he sees that he may belong also to other parents, and to friends of the parents. He may be brought into contact with the children of neighbors, with the children of friends of the parents, with children in pre-school groups or in church groups. As a result of the warm and affectionate relationship with the mother, he accepts other human beings as trustworthy and as "good people," and he learns that he, too, is expected to be friendly toward others and to find people whom he likes. Still later in his development, his parents would probably communicate some feeling of concern if he were alone all of the time, or if he weren't wanted by his age-mates. As the years pass by, he comes to realize that "belongingness" is to be prized; to be friendly toward others and to have others want you as a friend are normal expectations. He expects to be a part of the groups in which he is a member, and he expects to share with them and not be rejected by them. A need for belonging has been created, and here again, this is true only *if it is true!* In some family situations and in later years, children may grow up in circumstances where attitudes toward other people are characterized by suspicion or hostility. There may be parents who indoctrinate their children with the idea of rejection of others, of not being friendly to people in general. Where this situation obtains, the child's need for belongingness is thwarted. The consequences of this thwarting are reflected in the way he behaves.

Still another characteristic of the relationships between mother and child in the early days of infancy is the elimination of, or at least the reduction of, the feeling of fear. There is, in fact, an over-protection with respect to fears—as a general rule. Quite unconsciously, the mother knows that it is not good to frighten the little infant. Situations sometimes occur in which her wishes in this respect are denied, and when this happens she is greatly concerned. She wants her child to be relatively unafraid, to be able to stand up for himself, to be independent and to be venturesome in a variety of ways, and she knows almost instinctively that a fearful child will not behave in these ways. If older children in the family, relatives, children in the neighborhood, or visitors create situations that strike fear into the heart of the little youngster, the mother will remonstrate and point out the possible harm that could be caused. As her child grows up, the mother tries to help him to see the difference between fear and caution. At certain stages of his life she wants him to be cautious in using the scissors, but she does not want him to be afraid of them. She wants him to be cautious about climbing in high places, but she doesn't want him to be afraid of venturing off the floor. In hundreds of ways, the child learns from his mother that she will not frighten or scare him. He learns to be free of fear; he learns to have a need to be free from fear. As time passes, he comes to expect it almost as his right. Where this has been accomplished, the child is a more independent and self-respecting person. He uses his personality to explore the world around him, and to be a person in his own right, without the anxieties and doubts that are aroused by fear. Where, however, the control and direction of his behavior is largely motivated by fear, the child's need for inner security is again threatened. He is unable to function as an independent personality, as a trusting person, and the anxieties produced by fear are reflected in undesirable behavior.

Thus far mention has been made of the need for love and affection, the need for achievement and recognition, the need for economic security, the need for belonging, and the need to be relatively free from fear. There are a few more such emotional needs for children which are of great importance in the teaching-learning process. One of these has to do with the need to be relatively free from intense feelings of guilt. After the first year of life, many children begin to explore their environment and the world in which they live, with a confidence that is born in the relationships they have had in the past with their parents. As they grow older, this exploration of theirs brings them into contact with many aspects of the world in which they live, and as they meet these new situations they react to them, and often on a basis of inadequate knowledge and inadequate past experience. Parents who are impatient with habits relating to eating or toilet training might shame their children deeply. A child might show a naive hostility toward his parents and be disgraced by them because of revealing his feelings. In later months, children might use words that they have heard other children use, and they might be humiliated, shamed, and embarrassed by adults for using such expressions. In the exploration of their own bodies, or the bodies of their age-mates, children do things that are not sanctioned by adult standards. Under these innocent circumstances, some children are driven to a deep sense of guilt by parents who do not understand what they themselves are doing.

A similar kind of thing often happens with respect to the abuse or the destruction of property. The small child may not have developed an adequate sense of "mine and thine." When he takes money or some material object that belongs to somebody else, people near him may give him the sense of having committed a rather horrible crime. Under a combination or repetition of these circumstances, the child learns to have a feeling of guilt. He feels unworthy; he feels that he is not as good as his parents, or as good as other people; he begins to lose respect for himself. He feels mean and "low down."

Contrast this with the opposing tendency where one finds parents who understand that a child who is exploring the world will often say and do things that are unconventional. They help him to see that this is a new experience for him and offer to prepare him for these experiences as best they can. Over and over again, in perhaps hundreds of different situations, they help him to see that he did what he did because the situation was new and because he probably did not know how to handle it. They help him with the skills and understandings necessary to "size up" new situations. Where the child may have done something that was at odds with the prevailing code, and some other person nearby attempts to humiliate or to embarrass or to shame the child, they rush in to explain that this kind of treatment is not good for their child; they hasten to add that it is not a fault of the child, that it deals with his unawareness of what the situation required. They want to help their child to comprehend the environment. They don't want people to demean the child in his own estimate. They want their child to grow up with a certain pride in himself, a respect for himself, and a willingness to explore new situations without a feeling that individuals concerned with that exploration will seize opportunities to belittle children. It is under these circumstances that one *learns* to have the need to be relatively free from guilt. In this volume it is maintained that significant differences in behavior are to be expected from children who have a deep feeling of guilt when compared with children who do not have such a feeling.

The child and his mother in their relationships to each other are continually testing each other for the emergence of new and different patterns of behavior. In an overwhelmingly large number of families, the growing child is given many opportunities for choice. This is often true with respect to foods in the second year of life, or the clothes that a child will wear on a particular day. It pertains to where he will walk or whether he wants to ride or what toys he wishes to play with. In these early days of developing independence, the child *learns* from these relationships that he can expect to have some liberty in making choices that exist in the environment or that he can conceive of. He comes to feel that he should have some share in creating the values by which his activities shall be directed. Sometimes these choices occur in family group situations, and he is consulted about his wishes in a number of things. As the months go by, he seems to *learn* that he has a need for self-respect and for an opportunity to express himself in situations where he himself is concerned. This need for sharing in decisions, for expressing choices, for self-respect in arriving at group decisions is probably just as much *learned* as any of the other needs mentioned.

If in a number of situations in his early years he is given the impression over and over again that he doesn't count, that he should do what he is told, that his ideas are no good, that his wishes are of no importance, that he is too young, or too little, or not bright enough yet to participate in the making of a decision that affects him, this need to express his own values will be thwarted. It is a central argument of this volume that a child who has been started off by having his own choices considered and who has felt himself to be a part of a decision-making group will feel more secure and his behavior will reflect this. It is also contended that children who do not have the opportunity to express their values, to make known their choices, to share in decision-making will feel thwarted or frustrated and that their behavior will reflect this frustration. In another section, the consequences of the frustration of these needs will be discussed.

For those of us who teach, there is an eighth need that seems to be indoctrinated into children and with which we must be deeply concerned. At that stage of his development where the growing child begins to get some command of language, his questions pertaining to the world around him are seemingly endless and are not only tolerated, but rewarded, and he is thus encouraged to ask even more. It is a frequently commented upon characteristic of early childhood that it is a period of endless questioning. The fact that these questions persist, and even multiply, is an almost sure indication that an environment has been created in which the children feel free to raise these questions. The world seems to be something that they can be curious about, and, moreover, the permissiveness of the situation seems to result in a feeling that questions are normal and expected. This questioning is again quite obviously related to the inner security of children. Answers to questions as such may not contribute to security. If they did, the libraries, which contain thousands of answers, would be a natural habitat of school-age children. These questions arise out of the experiences of children, are asked spontaneously, and answers are expected immediately. The way in which the answers are given and the context in which the questions arise seem to be significant with respect to security on many occasions. It is important for the child to trust and respect those who supply his answers. The child seems to be seeing *himself* in relationship to the world around him. He seems to be trying to make some order, *his* order, out of the chaos that surrounds him. He seems to be extending the idea of purpose. His questions reflect a concern about comprehending life *as he perceives it.*

As the years go by, his questions often become bothersome. He wants to know why there are some people who are awfully rich and others who are awfully poor, why people get sick and why they die. He wants to know more about the God he has heard about, about the sun and the moon and the stars. He wants to know *his place* in the world of things. He wants to know why people are sent to prison. He wants to know about divorces. In fact, he wants to know so many things that before too long his mother at times becomes impatient with him, and she is apt to say, "Pretty soon now you will be in school and there the teacher will help you with all these questions of yours."

It may be an expectation of both mother and child that his concerns will indeed be given serious consideration when he goes to the elementary school. Given situations in which his questions may tumble out, given the freedom where he can discover the purposes of other people and the answers to many of his problems, the child grows into a sturdy, reliant member of society. He comes to understand the world better and his place in it. He comes to see that knowledge can be gained, that study habits can direct him, that many resources are available, and that for many, many questions there are reassuring answers or alternatives. This feeling that there is order in the world, that it is comprehensible, that he is expected to explore it, that there are resources to help him, and that his purposes will be clarified for him as he carries on the exploration, all of this comes to constitute "a natural right" or "a basic need" as time goes by.

Where his questions are given the silent treatment, where his questions are reinterpreted and then answered in such a way as to be meaningless to him, where his own concerns are not given consideration, and where he, instead, is always asked to find answers to questions which the teacher thinks are important are ways of frustrating this need for security in understanding the world and *his place in it.* Most children seem to grow up with this need for purposeful action. They try to find a place for themselves and for their energies, and they want their activities guided by some purpose that is intelligible to them. The child-rearing process has left them with an emotional need to feel secure in a world they are trying to understand, a world which by their efforts they are trying to influence in directions that make sense to them. It is the underlying thesis of this book that children who have this need fulfilled in life behave quite differently from those children who have it thwarted.

Before we conclude this section of the volume it may be well to recapitulate some of the theory. In the parent-child relationships a number of emotional needs seem to be created as the early child training is directed toward healthy growth and development. Children come to want and to expect love and affection; they want and need a feeling of achievement and recognition; they learn to need economic security; they come to need relative freedom from intense feelings of fear and guilt; they come to accept as a fundamental right a feeling of belongingness; they come to expect opportunities to express their choices where group decisions are being made, and to develop as people who want to have purpose in relationship to an understanding of the world around them. These needs, it is believed, are in large part indoctrinated by the parents and the culture in which the child lives. Where these needs are substantially satisfied, healthy growth and development takes place. Where they are thwarted, unhealthy developments are likely to occur.

A second part of the theory states that whereas these needs are often met in early childhood, there are many family situations in which the child rearing is one of inconsistency and doubt, even of rejection, and the child gets a relatively bad start. It is maintained that even under circumstances where the start is good, these needs are not thereby fulfilled for life. Throughout all the days of all the years that remain in the life span, every individual child, every individual person has the job of relating himself to the environment in such a way as to *try* to meet these needs. The job is a continuing one. Situations may come up on any day in which some of these needs may be seriously frustrated. Given a good start in life and continuing experiences of security, a person is better able to meet the frustrating situation. On the other hand, crucial situations may develop in which one or more of these needs are intensified and threaten the basic security of the individual. All those who work with children have a responsibility for recognizing the tremendous importance of these needs in healthy growth and development. All those who have responsibility for guiding the growth and development of children have the obligation also to understand what happens when these needs are thwarted. We may now turn to a consideration of the probable consequences of thwarting these needs.

3

BEHAVIORAL RESULTS OF FRUSTRATION

THE NEEDS THEORY

As teachers we know that there is no single, simple explanation for the extremely varied behavior of children. Most of us operate on the assumption that all behavior is caused; that if we are now unaware of some of these causal sequences, it is largely because of our present ignorance. We seem to believe that by studying behavior and studying man we can continue to find out much more about what makes him behave the way he does.

For all those interested in knowing more about the behavior of children and of adults, a most significant book was published in 1939. Its title: *Frustration and Aggression.*[1] It was produced by a team of scholars at Yale University, and it presented the daring hypothesis that aggression is always a consequence of frustration. They say that aggressive behavior always presupposes the existence of frustration and, contrariwise, that the existence of frustration always leads to some form of aggression.

Building upon the Dollard hypothesis, we may go farther and say that there are four additional "gross" manifestations of behavior

---

[1]John Dollard, et al. *Frustration and Aggression* (New Haven: Yale University Press, 1939).

which are indicative of frustration. In many instances, when children are frequently, almost continually, *submissive,* we may find that some of their emotional needs are not being met. Likewise, when a child frequently tends to *withdraw from the group,* from contact with others, it suggests that some deep-seated emotional needs are not being met. In recent years, much research has been done in the field of psychosomatic medicine. The studies of Dunbar[2] and others indicate that *many symptoms of physical illness have emotional concomitants.* This, then, is our fourth category of "gross" manifestations of behavior, that of psychosomatic symptoms of illness. The fifth relates to children whose behavior regresses to an earlier stage of development: a first grade child acting and perhaps talking like a three-year-old.

To sum up: We believe that frustration of emotional needs tends to show itself in five general types of behaviors; i.e., aggression, submission, withdrawing, psychosomatic symptoms of illness, and regression. Note, I have not stated that anyone who is frustrated acts in these five ways, but rather that anyone who acts in these five ways *may* be frustrated. In other words, these five types of behavioral symptoms indicate that emotional needs are probably not being met. We recognize this by these "gross" behaviors.

FRUSTRATION AND AGGRESSIVE BEHAVIOR

Teachers must be especially sensitive to the fact that any *one* of the following behaviors is not by itself indicative of aggression or of an unmet need. All children display aggression in some form or another and at various times. We are here trying to point up the behavior of a child who is more or less characteristically aggressive. We are looking for children who tend on many occasions and in various situations to show behaviors of the kind described below. We realize, of course, that some aggression is constructively channeled through the very work that we do. Some children have pent-up energy which they expend in ordinary games and sports or in scholastic competency and thus release this aggression in a way which is not harmful to other people or to property as such or to themselves.

For our present purposes, attention must be focused on a rather consistent pattern of aggressive activities, *with hostility involved;* on the child who more or less habitually tends to engage in the acts which we are here calling aggressive *in an unsocial manner.* We

---

[2]Helen Flanders Dunbar, *Mind and Body,* new enl. ed. (New York: Random House, Inc., 1955).

should note again that where these acts seem to appear rather continually and with more than mild intensity, the teacher is immediately warned that perhaps some emotional needs are not being met. The behavior as such does not point to any single or particular need. The behavior is of a "gross" kind; it merely serves to alert the sensitive teacher to the fact that children who behave in this fashion are children who may be troubled inwardly.

Some children reveal aggression in their language—in name-calling, swearing, loud yelling, domineering talk, talk of what they are going to do to some other people, statements indicating resentment toward the authority of adults, parents, age-mates, brothers and sisters, minority groups. "I don't like you," and "I hate you" are often expressions of rejection of others.

We sometimes hear children talk of revenge for real or imagined hurts by others, "getting back at somebody." Ofttimes we hear children bragging and making claims of superiority. The topics that children talk about are sometimes revealing: killing, murder, mysteries, war, torture, and various other cruelties. Aggression is often revealed in the overt actions of children: some children push, pull, tug or wrestle, hit, slap, punch or kick. Some throw things at others. Sometimes they carry or brandish guns or knives or other weapons.

Aggression is often directed toward property, e.g., cutting desks or writing on them, breaking chairs, or writing on walls. Aggressive children might even carry on what seems to be a planned program of waste of school property, their own property, or the property of others. Letting the air out of or puncturing automobile tires is another form of aggression directed against property. Some children soil or tear their own clothing or the clothing of others. Some children seem to be "getting back" at their parents by frequently losing some of their clothing or some of their possessions: toys, bicycle, books, etc. The movements of some aggressive children might be described as quick, decisive, jerky. Sometimes for no very obvious reason they tease other children or take things away from them or in other ways use people as scapegoats. Sometimes they show extreme cruelty to animals. In their relationships to teachers they are sometimes impudent or impertinent. Some seem to carry a chip on their shoulder. These aggressive children are quarrelsome and belligerent so often that they are recognized as the outstanding problems in the group.

For classroom teachers, aggressive behavior on the part of children constitutes a major problem. In the first place, it tends to disrupt the smooth working of the classroom group. Hence, it interferes with teaching and tends to make teaching more difficult. Second, it creates discipline problems and these have further consequences of many kinds, most of them bad. Third, the aggressive child is behaving in ways which make it more difficult for *him* to learn. Although behavior problems which involve aggression seem to be the most difficult for teachers to handle, the work of Dollard and his colleagues seems to offer a starting point for working with these children.

The question was: If aggression is always preceded by frustration, and if frustration is always followed by aggression, isn't it possible to find out what is frustrating some of these aggressive children, and couldn't we do something about it? And if we try to do something about it, will the aggressive behavior decline in intensity, or in frequency of happening, or both?

Beginning in the late twenties, and instigated largely by the writings of Freud, many scholars in the fields of education and psychology were studying an area which might loosely be called "The Needs of Children." Dr. Caroline Zachry and Dr. Alice Keliher headed commissions which were putting an emphasis upon *needs*. Was it possible or probable that certain needs of children were being frustrated, and that aggression was a consequence of this kind of frustration? The question seemed worth trying as an hypothesis, and much experimental work was carried on during the ensuing twenty-five years. In large measure the Dollard hypothesis was supported, and teachers tended to accept the idea as a starting point for working with aggressive children.

If *needs* were being frustrated—which needs? And how did one find out? There seemed to be substantial agreement on a number of these needs. It was widely accepted that human beings need love; that they need a sense of belonging, of identification with other humans; that they need a sense of achievement; that they need to be relatively free from deep feelings of fear and guilt; that they need a feeling of self-respect and power. Perhaps the Great Depression of the thirties suggested the need for economic security, and the increasing interest in psychoanalysis and psychotherapy may have suggested the need for understanding of self.

There was little agreement among those who made such lists of needs. One distinguished psychologist included forty-one needs in his statement, and among them he included the need for aggression! This latter point of view is receiving a great deal of support recently, from several fields of science. Lorenz[3] believes that some of man's

---

[3]Konrad Lorenz, *On Aggression* (New York: Harcourt, Brace and World, Inc., 1966).

undesirable behavior is the consequence of undischarged aggression, and he supports the view that a disposition to be aggressive is instinctive with man, as it is with most other animals. The same general outlook is interestingly and entertainingly put forward by Robert Ardrey.[4] Teachers should have access to these books in the professional library of every school. They present facts, inferences, and generalizations which are not often found in texts written for the teaching profession, and what they have to say deserves careful consideration.

Ardrey has much to say about conditions which promote amity within a group. He sees a very definite need for *enemies,* and for surrounding *hazards.* As hazards decrease, the enemy factor must increase if the same amount of amity is to be preserved. He sets forth this formula with much qualification, but he is grimly serious as he elucidates the concept.

Both writers lean heavily upon analogies to other animals, but Lorenz is much more cautious in his conclusions. Both make much of "instinctive" behavior patterns which suggest, in the case of man, *a* human nature that is pretty much unchangeable. In a chapter entitled "Avowal of Optimism," Lorenz indicates four or five alternatives for controlling some of the negative effects of aggression. No one of these suggestions is new, but as a whole they are a recognition that it is possible to control or to channel the aggressive drive into many kinds of behavior.

Another view of this whole matter is summed up by saying that aggression is learned, while a third view says it isn't the aggression that is learned, but the kind of aggression that will satisfy the feeling of frustration. This suggests that in different situations and at different epochs of man's history, certain kinds of aggressive responses are acceptable, and that in other times and places they are not. This opens very wide the door of reconstructing our present human nature. It suggests the possibility that we can create satisfactory substitutes for the more unwanted forms of aggression, including war itself. If such possibilities do indeed exist for modifying behavior, it can be surmised that much importance must be attached to the environment surrounding—let us say—the aggressive child. Most of us who teach tend to take this point of view.

For "instinct" I tend to use a softer word: "impulse." One measure of civilized man is related to his conscious and perhaps unconscious control of his impulses. He learns to mediate the "instinctive" drive;

---

[4]Robert Ardrey, *The Territorial Imperative* (New York: Atheneum, 1966).

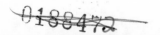

he pauses; he looks for alternatives; he may anticipate consequences. As he canvasses possibilities and looks to future consequences, he may choose not to act upon the impulse. As he does this over and over and over again, he forms the habit of so doing, and the life of impulse will no longer be all-pervasive, completely dominant. And this does not mean that "mind," the "intellect," has taken over.

In the total history of mankind, disciplined thinking is very recent. Even more recent is a regard for the values which are involved in almost every so-called thinking situation. As our schools and colleges and universities place more emphasis upon thinking situations, and as parents do so also, we may indeed significantly influence how we behave in a great many situations which once upon a time we responded to in terms of instinct or impulse.

Also, as we make a serious effort to clarify our values, as we help young people to know themselves, and as we get out into the open our conflicts with others that are value-centered, we are beginning to pay attention to values, and we tend to have some respect for the values of others. It isn't intellect alone that is mediating an impulse. It is a man or woman, boy or girl, responding to a situation as a total person.

Our concern in the area of aggression is not only with its origins: Is it inherited? Is it mostly learned? Can human beings learn new ways of channelizing the energy and/or the disposition which expresses the aggression?

Our concern as professional teachers is represented by the question: Can we do something to help children who are aggressive?

If our theory has some logical support, the aggression that shows up in behavior may be a symptom of an underlying emotional need that has been frustrated. If this is a reasonable hypothesis, it would then follow that our attention should not be directed toward treating this symptom, or trying to suppress it. Our concern would be with an effort to find out if some emotional needs are not being met and then to try to meet those needs. This kind of thinking is based on the assumption that if efforts were made to meet the aggressive child's emotional needs, we might expect a change in his behavior, resulting in a significant reduction in the aggressive symptoms.

On many occasions in the past, however, we teachers have not had a clear theory to operate on. We haven't understood the possible relationship between aggression and unmet needs, and we have tried to put an end to the aggression. Sometimes, of course, this is absolutely necessary for the health and safety of the child himself and other children. In a larger sense, however, this is more or less a doctrine of retaliation. We punish the child for his aggressiveness rather than make an attempt to understand the causes and try to treat those causes. We would not say of a sixteen-year-old child who had a temperature of 103° that he should put some ice in his mouth along with the thermometer; nor do we say to him that he is too old to have a temperature. We have come to learn something about bodily temperature; we have come to know what is normal and what is abnormal; and we understand that a very high temperature is symptomatic of something. Moreover, we have learned that this symptom needs to be related to some cause, and we want the child to go to a specialist who can investigate the cause. Within the profession of education, we can begin to formulate some theories relating to behavior that will be helpful to us in treating the causes of aggression. We do not know in any positive, scientific sense that every chronic case of aggressive behavior is due to frustrated emotional needs. We can, however, begin to investigate the behavior of a child *as if* some need may be frustrated. We may try to identify that need, and we may then try to do something about it. Where we see changes in behavior take place we can begin to have more confidence in the theory. Moreover, we shall probably build up a number of instances in which evidence of frustrated needs was related to evidence of aggressive behavior.[5] I am using the term frustration in the sense that we want something, or want to do something, and we are blocked or thwarted; we try and try again to achieve what we want, but it is denied us. Even so, we still want it and continue to want it. Wanting it so very much and being blocked, and still wanting it, we "take out" our feelings on people around us, or on property. If our parents represent the thwarting or frustrating personnel, we might lose or damage or destroy our own clothes or possessions, including toys and books and many other things in which our parents may have invested much money and pride. It is not possible for us to hit our parents; perhaps it is not even possible to defy them with impunity. Unconsciously perhaps, we strike at something they do value very much: property and prestige.

Let us suppose, for the moment, that a particular child has done just that; and let us also suppose that he feels neglected, unloved, even perhaps unwanted by his parents. He needs love and affection and warmth, a sense of trust in them, and wishes they would have such trust in him. He has, however, damaged or lost some valuable personal property. In the situation, although he needs most of all love

---

[5]We would not expect this to be true the other way around. In other words, we would not want to say that all aggression is the result of frustrated needs. We would expect, however, that some kinds of frustrated needs would lead to aggression.

and affection, he is hardly likely to get it. Forms of aggression, practically all of them, have the unfortunate quality of attracting responses which are additionally frustrating, and hence evoke still more expressions of aggression, and the circle goes round and round.

If we believe that behavior is caused, and if we accept the frustration-aggression hypothesis, and if with a particular child we sense that his aggression follows from the frustration of his deep-seated need for love, what should we try to do? I believe that we should try to bring love and affection to that child. How shall we know that his aggressive behavior points to a need for love? Later in this volume eight emotional needs have been chosen for description and analysis, among them the need for love, and it is assumed that these descriptions will be helpful in arriving at a tentative diagnosis. Even so, we must remember that educational diagnosis, not unlike medical diagnosis, involves artful guessing based upon our experiences with children and upon a thorough knowledge of what we are trying to do. We take the best hunch available, and we try it out. If it does not seem to be working, we try another.

Working with our colleagues, with graduate students, and all of us cooperating with hundreds of classroom teachers, we concentrated on *eight* emotional needs. We observed children in school and on the playgrounds. We talked with parents. We had many, many interviews with teachers about individual children. Out of these explorations, we decided to settle on these eight needs for further study.

1. the need for love and affection
2. the need for achievement
3. the need for belonging
4. the need for self-respect
5. the need to be free from deep feelings of guilt
6. the need to be free from deep feelings of fear
7. the need for economic security
8. the need for understanding of self

It should be immediately apparent that these eight do not exhaust a listing of the needs of boys and girls. There are indeed many more. These were chosen on the basis of several criteria: Most of them received frequent mention in the literature on the psychological needs of children; all eight can be related to behavior commonly expressed in school classrooms. A great many teachers chose them from a longer list as needs particularly important in terms of facilitating learning. They saw these eight needs as a minimum list to test the hypothesis that frustration of them might be associated with aggression, and with the four other consequences of frustration postulated in this volume:

1. evidences of withdrawing from social relationships
2. evidences of submissiveness
3. evidences of psychosomatic disturbance
4. evidences of regressive behavior

To test out any or all of these hypotheses several steps are involved. It is necessary, first of all, to identify an "aggressive" child. Then one must observe his behavior closely in an effort to determine what needs are not being adequately met. Third, it is necessary *to try to meet* those needs, and fourth, it is necessary to reassess the child's behavior to make a judgment about the effectiveness of this total approach.

These five ways of behaving we call *gross* manifestations of frustration. Children who characteristically behave in these ways are chosen for further study: An attempt is made to analyze their emotional needs, and behavior that seems to be closely related to a need is regarded as a *fine* manifestation. It is a kind of second screening. If the so-called *fine* manifestations do not show up, we decide that the child is NOT a needs case. We then look ever so much more closely into possible problems of physical health, into behavior associated with the absence of value development, and into problems associated with the child's status with his peers.

How does one make the decision that a child is characteristically aggressive? It is very difficult to describe the processes involved. We have outlined a number of behaviors ordinarily associated with "bad" aggressiveness. Experienced classroom teachers are sensitive to the fact that any single one of the behaviors is not by itself indicative of aggression or of an unmet need. The teacher looks for a child who tends on many occasions, and in a variety of situations, to show many of the behaviors we have associated with aggression. She is looking for a consistent and persistent pattern of these behaviors. She looks for a child who more or less habitually tends to reveal instances of aggressive behavior. Where they appear very frequently and with more than mild intensity, the teacher is immediately sensitive to the possibility that one or more emotional needs are not being met, and she undertakes the second step, the fine screening. The *gross* aggressive behaviors do not seem to point toward particular needs; they do, however, alert the teacher to the fact that children who behave in this fashion may indeed be troubled inwardly.

To accomplish the second step, the fine screening, the teacher should become familiar with all of the analyses of the eight emotional needs in chapter 3. She should make it a point to observe the child's behavior rather closely in terms of the descriptions made under each need. She makes a tentative diagnosis, and with this in mind, she continues to observe the child closely. If her earlier hunch is confirmed, she decides to proceed on that basis.

Now, she begins to make use of a form which appears below. She keeps this record for a period of two weeks, and then omits recording for three weeks. For another two weeks she records again, and she compares the two sets of records. From this comparison she formulates guides for her next steps.

HELPING TO MEET EMOTIONAL NEEDS
(Mimeograph this form)

Student's Name _____   Date _____

Check the needs you are trying to help this student to meet:

____ belonging   ____ love and affection
____ achievement   ____ freedom from fear
____ economic security   ____ self-respect
____ freedom from guilt   ____ self-understanding

1. In what ways, if any, were you able to reflect friendliness, security, self-confidence in your relations with this child today?

2. What situations, if any, developed in which this youngster received some criticism, or punishment, or rejection; or a sense of insecurity, pressure, tenseness or nervousness? Be brief.

3. Did any situations develop (other than in number one above) which tended to please the child, make the child more secure, more happy, more self-respecting? Perhaps other children helped him.

4. Was there anything different or unusual about the student's behavior today?

Keep this record daily for a period of two weeks. Then let it lapse for three weeks. Then go back to this daily recording for two weeks. Compare the two sets of records. Study these records as a guide for your next steps.

For carrying through the third step, an organized effort *to try to help* meet the needs of a particular child, the teacher makes almost daily use of that section of this volume entitled "Dos and Don'ts of the Needs Theory." Here she finds many suggestions directed toward the possible meeting of particular needs and a number of cautions about what to avoid.

There will be much more discussion of the many ideas which are involved in carrying out all of these steps in succeeding chapters, but before we get into those matters, there is some unfinished business in this chapter which must receive attention.

We have thus far presented the frustration-aggression hypothesis. We have described what is meant by aggressive behavior in the classroom, and we have indicated our meaning of frustration. We have also indicated other consequences of frustration: withdrawing types of behavior, submissiveness, psychosomatic symptoms, and regressive behavior. In the next few pages *gross behaviors* associated with these categories will be described.

If a child is characterized by these gross manifestations, the same steps are applied as were recommended in the case of aggression. One proceeds from the fine screening to a hypothesis about what needs are not being adequately met, and then makes an organized attempt to meet those needs.

FRUSTRATION AND SUBMISSION

We said that there are five types of behavior disturbances that occur in our classrooms which are of great concern to teachers. We took as our first kind the aggressive child, and we said that when emotional needs are thwarted, some children are apt to show this frustration in becoming aggressive toward others. Not all frustrated children, however, meet life situations by aggressive acts. Some children may have tried to be aggressive and did it under certain circumstances where they were punished severely. Some children whose needs are thwarted over a long period of time seem to give up. They lose spunk and backbone. They become unusually submissive. They seem "cowed." They seem to have little sense of direction for themselves. There is a tendency to look to other people for suggestions as to what to do, and when to do it, and where to do it, and when to stop doing it.

Here again I want to warn the reader that no child would engage in all of the following behaviors. One or two or even three of these behaviors are not necessarily indicative of chronic submissiveness.

Studies have shown that some children who have been aggressive in a situation where they were frustrated have met a rather severe kind of punishment and as a result these children seem to have lost their backbone.

If we were to look at the behavior indulged in by the child who is submissive, we would be apt to find that he has an unusual preference for old and familiar things; he is very timid about trying new things and is extremely hesitant in trying out new ideas. He is often afraid to meet new people and has serious difficulty in making his own decisions or choices. He rarely protests when he is pushed around and seldom fights back when picked on by other people. He seems to be quite easily frightened. He yields to authority with little hesitation or protest and rarely, if ever, disagrees with group opinion. Quite often he lets you know that he feels that the other children know much more and can do much better than he can. He often requires careful and specific advice in order to direct his behavior. Often he is afraid to play rough games. Sometimes he cries rather easily, and once in a while we have the youngster who whines a lot. Amongst children he sometimes is referred to as a "sissy" or a "goody-goody." He seems to be afraid of making mistakes. His feelings are often hurt. He doesn't engage in competition as a rule and seems to show considerable dependence on other people. The submissive child is very often unobtrusive and undemanding. He is frequently imitative. He tends to take the path of least resistance. He seldom ventures to volunteer in class and is very timid in reporting before groups. If he gets in trouble, he is usually led into it by others.

If we turn for the moment to the things that other people are likely to do for and to the submissive child, we notice that he is pushed quite frequently by other people. The submissive child's opinions are not often solicited. If he has questions to ask, often they are neglected or avoided or rejected. Sometimes he is used as a scapegoat by some of the more aggressive children. It is not uncommon to find that the submissive child is not accepted by the group. The group often belittles his accomplishments if he shows any. He is criticized a great deal and is sometimes picked on and teased by the others. If any promises are made to a child of this sort, it is not uncommon to find that the promises are not kept. Others tend to expect a lot of obedience from him, and after a while one often hears other children nagging him or mimicking him or exploiting him excessively.

If we turn to the relations that he may have with other people, we find that the submissive child tends to have very few and sometimes no real companions. He may try to win his way by flattery, by toadying to others, or by manipulation of people. He sometimes gets his way by wheedling, begging, or crying. As his submissive behavior continues, it is common to find that even the parents lose interest in the child, and teachers tend not to know that he is in the room. Once in a while we find teachers and parents who are overindulgent to this child, who tend to baby him a great deal. If we were to inquire into his out-of-school behavior, we might find that he does not sleep very well. In general adults wish that he had more gumption, more backbone, more self-direction, more spirit. Sometimes his talk reflects a maturity which suggests that he is trying to relate himself to adult society, and this is frequently the outcome of not being able to make friends with his own age-mates.

If we were to observe the submissive child for certain physical symptoms, we probably would notice that he blushes easily and rather often. We might find that he bites his nails or sucks his thumb or covers his mouth with his hand when speaking. We might find some tenseness in the body, some rigidity when he is called upon to do something before the group. We may see a certain twitching of the fingers or a blinking of the eyes. We might find a child who does a lot of fiddling with his fingers or his hands or his clothes. In all of these ways we see evidences of a child who has become submissive in his relationships to other people—his age-mates and the adults in the immediate society.

The point being made here is that these submissive children are also children who may have emotional needs that are not being met, and that if we tried to meet these needs, their submissive behavior would probably change. They would probably become somewhat more assertive and would be inclined to participate in the affairs of the group. If we were successful, we probably would notice that the submissive child would change in such a way that he would not be pushed around quite so frequently by other people. He would have more questions to ask, and his opinions would tend to be solicited. He would not be used as a scapegoat by some of the more aggressive children, and he would come to be accepted more by the classroom group. Instead of belittling his accomplishments, as often happens, the group would probably reduce its criticisms. There would be more respect for him than he received theretofore, and less nagging or teasing. If we were successful in meeting his needs, the very submissive child would probably decrease the amount of flattery that he now employs. He would toady less to others and would be less easily manipulated by other students. We would expect a decrease in wheedling or crying. As he began to "perk up," we might expect children and parents and teachers to take a greater interest in him and begin to be aware of his presence. We might learn that he was sleeping better than he did, and his parents or his age-mates might report that he had more gumption, more backbone, more spirit than before. We should expect that he would be less likely to find his companionship with older people or with children much younger than himself, and that he would be more and more in the company of his age-mates.

As we work with the submissive child, trying to meet his needs, we might observe some changes in physical symptoms. It is possible that we might notice that a child blushes much less frequently. Our observations might indicate that he bites his nails less, is beginning to give up sucking his thumb. There may be less rigidity, less tenseness, and more relaxation when he is working with others. Certain twitching of the fingers or blinking of the eyes might begin to diminish. There would be less fiddling with his fingers or his hands, or his clothes.

In this section we have tried to paint a picture of the typically submissive child, what he does and what might happen if some of his emotional needs are met. We should review the main points. Partly through heredity but largely through environment, children *learn* to have certain emotional needs. When these needs are met, we have a kind of normal behavior and good mental health. When they are not met, some children become aggressive in their behavior. Not all children do this, however; some children instead become very submissive. They, too, often suffer from unmet emotional needs. The theory suggests that if we could meet the needs of the aggressive child, his aggressive behavior would decline. The theory suggests that if we could meet the needs of the submissive child, more assertive behavior would be a consequence. There are other types of behavior problems to which we must now turn.

FRUSTRATION AND WITHDRAWING TYPES OF BEHAVIOR

"Withdrawing" seems to be a way of life with some children. With others it is submissiveness; with still others it is a persistent, consistent kind of aggression. Why the different reactions? We really don't know—they may be related to hereditary factors, to body build, to the family constellations; it may be the result of accidental behavior in some crucial situations. A child may have received much more loving attention and care when he was belligerent: The behavior was reinforced and, with repetition, became a habit. Another child may have tried aggressiveness, and may have been severely punished for it. A random choice of meek submissiveness may have been greatly rewarded and, when repeated, rewarded again. Habits can and do start in these ways, quite by chance, and dispositions to withdraw from social contacts may have a similar origin. We can only guess about probable origins and possible causes, but we really do not know.

There are some children who choose neither aggression nor submission as ways of expressing their frustration. Instead they tend toward a solitary type of behavior, toward withdrawal from society. These children tend to shun contact with their fellows. They very often play by themselves, and they are not chosen by the group as members of committees or as teammates. They are not chosen to participate in games, and very often these children walk to school and home alone. When the schedule of the school calls for a period of recess, we often find the children who withdraw remaining in their seats. Sometimes if the schedule requires them to go outside, they will dawdle within the school. It will take them a long time to get their desks in shape before they can go out for recess, or they might go to the toilet and linger there for a while, thus making it impossible to have any kind of lengthy contact with other children on the playground. Sometimes these children take a seat in the classroom that isolates them from others, or sometimes we see them hovering on the fringe of group activities but declining to participate. Over and over again they seem to prefer spectator activity rather than participatory activity. One of the artful ways by which self-isolation is achieved may frequently be observed in a kind of specialization which such a child may develop. He or she will spend an enormous amount of time building model airplanes or drawing scenes that are complex and difficult or in fashioning elaborate costumes for dolls. As he spends more and more time at such an activity that isolates him from others, he is apt to develop special competence and skills in the things on which he is concentrating. It is not uncommon to find teachers and parents, too, who commend the child so highly for this specialty that it motivates him to spend more time at the skill, and he is actually encouraged to stay away from the group more even than is his wont.

In this same category we should include those children who want very much to belong to the group, but for some reason or other are rejected. They may be unskilled and awkward, come from "the wrong families," or have disfigurations that are unseemly, etc., etc. This tendency of the child to be by himself, to prefer the association of adults rather than his age-mates, to engage in activity which in a quite natural way divorces him from others, to be on the fringe of things and never in the center of them, to tend to resist the attempts of some well-intentioned adults to get him to participate—all of these are behaviors that are symptomatic of a withdrawing type of child.

The needs theory suggests that this solitary type of behavior may be a consequence of unmet emotional needs. If we knew how to identify some of these needs and if we tried to meet them, the theory implies that the child would become a more vigorous, a more participating member of the classroom group. Instead of remaining on the fringe of activities, there would be a tendency to become an interacting member of the group. Instead of contenting himself with solitary interests, he would begin to interest himself in things that are also pleasures of other people. If our efforts to meet his needs are successful, he probably will talk more to other children, he probably will find someone to walk home with, or he may invite a child, or even several children, to his home. He may initiate the idea of wanting to go to the movies with others, or to accompany them to athletic events. As our attempts to meet his needs are successful, we would expect him to merge with the group more and more. He would not "stick out" as an isolate.

We have said that when emotional needs are frustrated, some children become aggressive and some become very submissive. In this section we have said that some children whose emotional needs are not being met tend to withdraw, to become isolates or fringers. We do not mean to say that every child who is an isolate does have unmet emotional needs. There is a strong possibility that some of these children live a very rich inner life. Some of them are unusually imaginative and creative. They derive great satisfaction in expressing this creativeness in activities which other children cannot share. Some of these typically solitary children have one friend, and for them this seems to be adequate. The discerning teacher can detect in the behavior of the isolate whether the solitary behavior is one of great pleasure to the child himself, or whether it is a retreat from some kind of conflict. The carefully observant teacher will be able to note if the solitary child seems to be unusually happy in his relative isolation. We are concerned here only with those extreme examples of isolation in which there seems to be some evidence that inner security has not been met. We believe that many children who are "fringers," who are isolates, are children whose emotional needs are not being met, and that if we tried to meet those needs, these children would find great satisfaction in more shared activities with their age-mates.

FRUSTRATION AND REGRESSIVE BEHAVIOR

In some previously published materials, I did not make a separate category of these behaviors. Continuing contact with teachers in the field suggests that this type of behavior is on the rise in frequency and as a source of difficulty in classroom management. By regressive behavior I mean a return to behavior that is more characteristic of an earlier age. To "act like a baby," or to act like "a four-year old," to use some common expressions, is to indulge in regressive behavior. I associate these behaviors with some emotional difficulty that may have intruded very recently, and I hypothesize that one or more emotional needs are not being met.

This is another of the five *gross* symptoms of frustration. Assuming that you are a kindergarten teacher, you may notice one day that a child is acting very much like a three-year-old. For the next several weeks you may see evidences of very early childhood behavior on the part of this particular child. She cries a good deal, she may want to sit on your lap, she may call you "Mommie" on a number of occasions, she may start to lisp in her talking or revert to other infantile patterns of speaking. She may want help or assistance from you on tasks which you *know* she can do very well by herself. She may tug on your dress, want to hold your hand, and may crave for almost continuing attention.

If you are a teacher of fourth or fifth grade you may see a child regress to the behavior of a kindergartner or of a first grader. He may want to play only with younger children, or only with little girls. He may choose to play with toys that seem appropriate for a much younger child. He may even perform at a much lower level in reading and in arithmetic. You *know* that his achievement level is much higher, and you may be astounded at this change in his behavior. He has *regressed* to an earlier stage of development. I believe that *regression* that persists for some time is an expression of unmet emotional needs, that it is one way of reacting to frustration. Here again, many children will on occasion revert to an earlier stage of development. We are trying to identify the child who is persisting in this kind of behavior.

With very young children of school age, this may be shown by a loss of control of toilet habits previously well established. Some of these very young children will indicate that they cannot put on their own rubbers or overshoes or coats: They want help. The teacher knows that these simple tasks had been mastered, and she wonders about this new dependence and these symptoms of regression.

Some will indulge in "baby talk" again. Some will whine and cry over practically nothing. Others will pretend that they cannot read or do the simple sums which they had learned. Again, they seem to want help and attention.

Others seem to want warm body contact. When they cry, it will be near the teacher, and they may put their head in your lap, or throw their arms around your neck and sob convulsively.

Some of these behaviors may also characterize the "regression" of older children. These may also engage in a lot of child-like giggling and, at times, child-like hysterical laughter. On occasion there is an abandonment of the responsibilities associated with their present age level. There seems to be a great deal of "forgetting"; they forget the rules, the assignments, their books for homework, excuses for absences, their hats or coats which were left on the playground, their gym clothes.

Sometimes the quality of their work regresses to that of an earlier grade level. They will be much more slovenly than usual. Little responsibility will be assumed for neatness or for organization. And this will constitute a departure from already established habits.

Some will want to play games that they used to play when much younger. Some will want to play only with younger children. Some will talk a great deal about the fun they had when they were in earlier grades, when "they were young."

Where there had been evidence of self-direction and good ability to follow instructions and suggestions, some children begin to demand almost "perpetual" care; they seem to want your total undivided attention, and they want it often. You see this, and many of the other behaviors, as *babyish,* as signs of immaturity. Are they, perhaps, GROSS symptoms of some unmet emotional needs? With these children should you try to make some analysis of the needs situation, and where the evidence suggests it, should you try to meet these needs?

FRUSTRATION AND SYMPTOMS OF ILLNESS (Psychosomatic)

By law, and by right, teachers are not supposed to attempt diagnoses of the impairment of physical health. This is the professional task of the professionally trained physician. Nothing in this section should be interpreted as a recommendation or a suggestion that teachers should try their hand at making medical diagnoses.

Even so, we recognize a responsibility on the part of the teacher to recognize gross symptoms of ill health, not to make a diagnosis, but to inform the parents, the school doctor and nurse, or the school principal of something that may require early medical attention. Retching and vomiting in the classroom or on the playground may be such a symptom; it may be most unusual behavior on the part of a boy or girl. There may be the appearance on the skin of blotches of various sizes, a fainting spell, or an epileptic attack. An unusually severe asthmatic experience may occur, or signs of unusually labored breathing. There may be clues from a child's expression of pain: pains in his head, in his ears, in his stomach, in his limbs. A child may develop a temperature much higher than normal, and a sensitive teacher may recognize that something is wrong and should have attention quickly.

All of these things can and may happen to children who are emotionally poised and stable. They are in all knowable ways normal children, and we would not ordinarily associate these symptoms of these children with frustrated emotional needs. There are symptoms, however, which occur with regularity at certain times of the daily school schedule which call for additional attention.

Sometimes parents are very helpful. They inform the teacher about matters of health, and the wise teacher makes careful notes of these statements. A parent of a very young child may say that in moments of stress her child, of kindergarten age, may have an upset stomach. Another parent comments on allergies, another on hay fever, and another on asthma, and perhaps all of them suggest that the seriousness of the symptom seems to increase with the pressures felt by the child in particular situations.

Some children, when frustrated, tend to brood and worry and wind up having some kind of physical impairment. These children are said to have psychosomatic illnesses. If we study carefully the work of Flanders Dunbar[6] and of Franz Alexander[7] and Leon Joseph Saul,[8] we will find that these psychosomatic disorders are of several kinds. In this classification, we have children who have skin diseases: eczema, rashes, and other symptoms that seem to be associated with allergies. There are children who seem to show symptoms of cardio-vascular disturbances. These children show signs of extreme hypertension and of palpitations at times. We have children with arthritis and forms of rheumatism. A kind of miscellaneous grouping is made up of children with migraine headaches, recurrent back or body

---

[6]Dunbar, *Mind and Body.*

[7]Franz Alexander, *Psychosomatic Medicine* (New York: W. W. Norton & Co., 1950).

[8]Leon Joseph Saul, *The Hostile Mind* (New York: Random House, Inc., 1956).

pains, or disturbances of the kidneys or bowels. We also may have students in our schools who reflect disturbances of the respiratory tract. Some of them have recurring attacks of hay fever. In the gastric type we have people who develop ulcers or children who might come down with colitis of one kind or another, or painful diarrhea with cramps often with mucous in the evacuation. Sometimes children will instead show symptoms of constipation. In another group we may include those children with various speech defects: those who stutter and stammer and those who lisp. We must add also those with tics of various kinds. Under this general heading of psychosomatic disturbances, Flanders Dunbar also includes the idea of "accidentitis"—the child who is an accident repeater. She includes also some tendencies toward tuberculosis and to cancer and has some evidence to indicate that sugar diabetes is not unrelated to the frustration of emotional needs. Children who have various symptoms of this kind seem to be not ill enough to be under a doctor's care in the home or in a hospital. On the other hand they don't seem to be well enough really to get along with their age-mates and to carry on the learning process. It should be said again that, as a general rule, no child has a large number of these symptoms. Moreover, it can be said of every child that at one time or another some such symptoms as these are present in his behavior. Again we are trying to picture the child who has a more or less *chronic* condition of this kind.

It should be emphasized here that we are not encouraging teachers to make a diagnosis of illness. In fact, it is specifically suggested that in this respect teachers should always call upon a physician for help if it is needed. In this section we are asking the teacher to be a very careful observer and to notice if these symptoms of illness are related to a child's classroom activities. For example, does the child's hay fever or asthma become more intense when there is some kind of pressure being applied in the classroom by the teacher or by other children? Do some children tend to show certain stomach disorders in the reading period, or the arithmetic period, or when recess time comes? Are there some children who find it necessary to leave the room at certain hours of the day? Do children complain of not feeling well when they have to make some kind of recitation or carry out certain kinds of participation?

It should be repeated that what is wanted here from the teacher is an observance of the relationship between these symptoms of illness and certain classroom situations. Where this relationship exists, it seems reasonable to conclude that threats exist to the inner security of the child. When these threats come into operation, the child "takes it out on his own body." He begins to feel sick, and the symptoms of illness become more obvious.

Many of us believe that there are quite a few cases like this in our classrooms. These children are not sick enough to stay at home, and yet they are often really too sick to be in school. The school curriculum as it is organized, the human relations within the groups, make so many demands upon these people which they cannot meet that their inner security is threatened, and the consequent behavior shows up in recurrent symptoms of physical impairment.

It should be remembered that in identifying these children, we are not looking for those who show the behavior only rarely. We are trying to identify children who have a more or less chronic condition of a certain kind. Where we find this outcropping of physical symptoms correlated with particular stresses in the classroom, we conclude that something must be done to try to meet the emotional needs of these children.

Evidence has accumulated to show that there are some people who are *accident-prone.* Repeatedly, they are involved in accidents. In her volume, *Mind and Body: Psychosomatic Medicine,* Helen Dunbar reports the results of her investigations in this area. Over and over again, the accident-prone persons seemed to have emotional problems, and the accidents were in some ways associated with these problems. In this case, of course, there would not be the correlation with time and subject, but if you do have an accident repeater among your students, it may be helpful to consider this behavior as another *gross* manifestation of one or more unmet emotional needs.

In all of these *gross* behaviors associated with psychosomatic illness, remember—you are not trying to heal the sick; you are not trying to cure the illness. You see a relationship between symptoms and the normal stresses of learning and living in school. For the children who particularly need it, you will be sensitive to this relationship, and you will be trying to reduce the stress. Secondly, because the hypothesis suggests a relationship between these gross behaviors and unmet emotional needs, you will try to make an analysis of the child's needs, and you will be making efforts to meet those needs. As you succeed in these efforts you will probably be making a significant contribution to the reduction of stress. A child who is more secure emotionally will be able to withstand more stress, including the pressures of normal daily living.

This chapter has concerned itself with some of the many consequences of the frustration of eight emotional needs. Discussions of aggressive types of behavior, submissive types of behavior, withdrawing types of behavior, regressive types of behavior, and a listing of many symptoms of psychosomatic illness were included. Along with each presentation there was the suggestion that the reader should scan all names in the class and identify those who seemed to fit a particular classification.

On several occasions you may have found that a child is characterized by more than one of these *gross* manifestations of unmet emotional needs. This has happened many times and is, perhaps, even more convincing evidence that the causes may lie in unmet emotional needs.

After investigating the *gross* manifestations of frustration, you were advised that the next step was to be one of a still finer screening. You were to look for clues which would probably suggest which ones of the eight emotional needs were not being met. To do this you will need to have some idea of the ways each of these needs could be reflected in the behavior of children. The next chapter describes in greater detail each one of the eight emotional needs.

4

DESCRIPTIONS
OF THE EIGHT
EMOTIONAL NEEDS

I. THE NEED FOR BELONGING

In this section we will be looking at the child who feels unwanted and neglected. He either does not have as many friends as he *wants* or he does not have friendships with the people he wants as friends. He feels left out, in some way rejected, or feels that something is wrong with him. He needs to belong, to be a part of the group. What are some of the symptoms of this type of child?

Let us first look at some of the things he says. In many different ways he may express a deep desire to become a member of a group. "Why can't I belong to that club or gang?" or "I'm never chosen for any committee" or "I wish somebody would ask me to go to the movies or someone's house" are expressions typical of such a child. We may hear him say: "Why are the kids always too busy to go places with me?" "No one ever calls me on the phone." In a number of other ways this lonely child expresses wishes for more friends when he says he wishes he were not alone so often, he wishes there were more kids living near home, or that he lived in a different neighborhood. It is not uncommon to hear him say, "I wish my parents would let me bring other kids into the house and have a good time the way other families do," or "I wish I had somebody to play with after school and on Saturdays." He may complain: "Every time I call up other kids to go some place with me they're too busy or they have something else to do or they just don't want to." He begins to think that he must be different from others, and so we sometimes hear him say, "I wish the other kids didn't think I'm different"; "I wish they wouldn't call me names and make fun of me"; "I wish I could play games well enough so that the other kids would want me on their team." Very often we hear the "sour grapes" kind of thing. Alone, deserted, rejected, the child says: "I don't want to belong anyway" or "I didn't want to do that anyhow" or "I don't care" or "I don't like those kids!" Have you heard these children say rather frequently: "They don't want me" or, plaintively, "I haven't any friends!"?

Many of us who teach do not "hear" children when they say things like the foregoing. We may be busy with other things; we may be listening for anything that pertains in some way to the curriculum as we understand it. We may, as yet, be somewhat insensitive to the needs of children, and particularly to the need for belonging. After all, the child is *in the group;* there are children all around him. Why should he feel lonesome and estranged? As a matter of fact, he is ringing a very loud bell. He is saying something that is very hard for a human being to say. He is saying to you: "I need help. I need a friend. I need to feel that I too belong to the group. Please help me. I'm in trouble."

This consuming need for belonging shows up in the way a child acts, also. Rejected by the group over and over again, this child tends to remain on the fringe of group activity; he often remains in his seat "preoccupied." He's the one who's looking on most of the time, hardly ever in the middle of things; he doesn't actively participate. This is the child who comes to school alone, who lingers behind as the others walk home, or is alone and perhaps last or first on the bus. He sometimes even crosses the street to avoid meeting other children.

This child, who may daydream a lot of the time, may also preoccupy himself with specialization of effort; he works very hard to achieve high grades, does a great deal of reading, spends a lot of time at a rather solitary hobby, or develops special skills, such as drawing, woodwork, model building, etc.

Sometimes this lonely child feels the need for belonging in such a way that he becomes aggressive; he may try to force his way into the group. When the group does ask him to join in their work or play, he may defiantly reject the invitation.

It is one of the strange characteristics of human relationships that where we have children with deep emotional needs, they are apt to have those needs deepened in their contacts with their fellows. In other words, the ordinary behavior in a group is apt to make already unwanted children even more unwanted. Let us see what teachers and other adults are likely to do to a child who has a need for belonging. Often at home there may be a tendency to get the child "out of the way." He may be sent away to private schools or camps or to live away from home; he may be told: "When our company comes, you stay in your room" (and when adult guests stay, he may be told to relinquish his bedroom). This child is very frequently left home with a baby sitter while he knows his parents are at the movies, or his entire personal care may be left to a housekeeper or maid. The teacher may send this child to the cloakroom, to the corridor, to the principal's office. She may put him at the foot of the line. Many of her criticisms might be personal and public. This child has often been told by some adult: "You're always following me around" or "Can't you play by yourself some time?" It is very disheartening for this child to hear, so much of the time: "I don't blame the kids for not liking you" or "You're not the type for that part."

Let us turn now to the possible feelings of the child with a need for belonging. Of course, no one person can be sure of how another person feels, but in this section we are asking for your best guesses. You have seen this child and you have heard him and you have some understanding of him. Do you think his feelings could be expressed in any of the following ways?

He seems lonely; he feels almost deserted; he does not have the feeling that someone is his very best friend. He does not feel that he has someone in whom he can confide his secret worries and his concerns and perhaps his secret ambitions; he feels that he is outside, left out. He has a general feeling of insecurity—his world is threatened; he senses that these things are known by adults and he feels further depressed. The feeling that no one wants him may bring demoralization. When praised for what he does and what he says, he feels almost like rejecting the praise; he wants to feel that somebody would welcome him almost regardless of any excellence that he might exhibit; he wants to feel that there is some place he can turn where he can feel almost sure of being welcomed. He wants above everything else to relax; wants to be one with the others; would like not always to be stretching himself to "get in" or make a good impression or to hold up his end. He would like to develop an atmosphere in which he could feel at ease rather than feel taut. He feels helpless; has a feeling of decreased personal worth; feels that other children are quite all right but he himself must in some strange way be different because he is not being accepted. He is "crying on the inside"; he is not needed; he is unwanted.

On a sheet which includes the names of all your children, enter in column one the frequency and intensity with which the need for belonging is manifested by the kinds of behaviors described above. Use the following scale: Do this only for the few children you plan to work with as "probable needs cases."

FREQUENCY	INTENSITY
1—every month or so	a—extremely mild symptoms
2—every few weeks	b—on the mild side
3—every week	c—mild toward severe
4—several times weekly	d—on the severe side
5—daily	e—serious disturbance
6—several times daily	f—extremely serious disturbance

II. THE NEED FOR ACHIEVEMENT

Some children seem to clamor for attention. They feel that they are overlooked, and want more praise and recognition than they are receiving. This happens even when teachers believe they are giving unusual amounts of time to a particular child. There is a deep need here for achievement, for successful effort, and for praise of both effort and accomplishment. These symptoms seem to be present in children with the emotional need in the following description.

The child expresses the wish to "do something" or "do more" or "do it better." We sometimes hear a child make excuses: "I could have done it all right if Mary hadn't bothered me" or "I could do all those things if only I had some nice crayons and paper." He may protest, "She always tells me I can't do it" or "I never get a chance to do anything around this school." In various ways, this child lets us know that other people treat him unjustly: "I wish people would notice the work I do." "I wish people wouldn't scold me so much." "She's always picking on me" (meaning teacher). And generally he has occasion to blame others for his failures.

The child with a deep need for achievement sometimes indicates that he thinks other people are smarter or superior to himself. He wishes he could do work like others; he wishes he could do his own work with less help from others—"Everybody else does better than I do." He boasts of the success of various members of his family. He ridicules the work of others. He reveals that he would like more praise; he says he wishes the teacher thought he was going to pass; he tries to bluff his way out of failures; he places disproportionate value on small achievements and calls attention to each of them. He reveals a genuine dissatisfaction with his own accomplishments: He says he wishes he knew how to study better; he wishes he could play an instrument and be in the school orchestra; he wishes he could play games better; he wishes he were improving in his school work; he wishes he could think of the right things to say. He rationalizes his failures, makes excuses, boasts of things he used to do, e.g., "I used to be on the honor roll." He indicates an antagonism toward his environment: He complains about his tools, his teacher, his school. He blames circumstances for his failures: "I can't get it; it's too hard." His work is uninteresting; he's bored. This child is likely also to say he is worried about an examination.

Children who are under the pressure of a need for achievement are apt to do things which indicate their emotional disturbance. Very often the child is likely to indicate a desire to shy away from any activity where his ability might be questioned. He avoids competitive situations; he cheats on examinations; he copies his homework. He associates with children several years younger or older than himself.

He may reveal a lack of ambition. There is no "will to learn." He is indecisive; he is lazy and indifferent; he refuses to recite. On the other hand, the child with a need for achievement often has a dogged determination to learn. He works very long or very hard in all activities; he spends time trying to do things beyond his powers; he "doesn't know when to give up." Sometimes he reveals aggressive qualities toward people and things. He sabotages or destroys the work of others; he tries to bluff his way.

We have said that an emotionally disturbed child is disturbed even more by what takes place in group situations. In other words, the aggressive child often invites retaliation when he needs therapy. Let us see what can happen to the child who has a need for achievement. When he is aggressive toward his age-mates, they react in like fashion. All the while he is suffering from lack of a sense of achievement, adults are likely to make comparisons such as these: "Johnny, why don't you get good grades like Tom does?" or "Your papers are never as neat as the other children's" or "Look how nicely Ted always picks up his things." Over and over again this child is told: "You never finish anything you start"; "Why do I always have to help you with your work?" and the almost classic, "I'm sure you can do better than that." Instead of praise, this child receives commands such as, "Stop daydreaming and try to accomplish something" and, frequently, "Don't give up so easily." Parents and teachers alike often contribute in other ways to the misery of the child with a need for achievement. "Picking on" or nagging the child in the presence of others tends to exaggerate emotional insecurity. Very often adults pay little or no attention to the child's achievements, and the child is seldom given a chance to show what he can do. We very often set goals which are too high for the child, and then compare him with someone who does much better work. Sometimes teachers do not give these children enough help, so that they have little chance to feel success, and on the other hand, many parents tend to keep such children so busy at home that they do not have any time for school work.

The child with a deep need for achievement may meet frustration at home, in the school, and on the playground. It is possible that the feelings of a child may be revealing. No one person can be certain of just how another person feels, but in this section we would like for you to make your best guesses. You have seen these children and you have heard them and you have some understanding of them. Is it possible that some of these statements express their feelings?

The child with a need for achievement may feel that he cannot do the required work; that too much is being asked of him; that he should be able to but can't. He feels depressed by repeated failure; he feels poorly prepared, inferior in skill, in achievement, or because of personal physique, habits, or character traits. He feels that his age-mates rate him low in ability; feels that he "could have done better," etc., and he is sometimes convinced that he will never amount to much.

On the sheet which includes the names of all your children, enter in column two the frequency and intensity with which the need for achievement is manifested by the kinds of behaviors described above. Use the following scale: Do this only for the few children you plan to work with as "probable needs cases."

FREQUENCY	INTENSITY
1—every month or so	a—extremely mild symptoms
2—every few weeks	b—on the mild side
3—every week	c—mild toward severe
4—several times weekly	d—on the severe side
5—daily	e—serious disturbance
6—several times daily	f—extremely serious disturbance

III. THE NEED FOR ECONOMIC SECURITY

We do not equate economic security with wealth or possessions. In this section we are trying to identify children who are disturbed or troubled because their economic situation (no matter how good or how bad) is *uncertain.* The immediate future is either confusing or threatening. They are worried for fear the present situation will be greatly changed. Sometimes these children worry "out loud," and we hear them say, "Maybe Daddy will get laid off" or "When I get old will I be poor like my grandma?" It is not unusual to hear children reflecting the worries of their parents as when a child might say, "Mommy said if Daddy gets sick she doesn't know what we'll do" or "Daddy said if we had any more children it would be hard to get all the things we need." We may hear children say things like this: "I need to go to the dentist but my Mommy says we'll have to wait. Maybe I won't ever get to go" or "Lots of times Daddy has promised to get us things and then something happens. Will it always be like this, that something will happen?" or "I was pretty sure I was going to get a new dress and then my brother got sick" and "Almost every time I want something, my parents say they can never tell what might happen." Frequently a child of this sort will worry about the prospect of moving; "If things don't get any better maybe we'll have to move." Sometimes we hear a child say, "We don't drive our car, because we don't know if something will happen to it." In other words, the child with the need for economic security is apt to make continued reference to his father's job, wages, or other economic factors which he feels may be threatened now or in the future. He generally lacks faith in the future.

In their actions these children often show symptoms of economic insecurity. Sometimes we see a child who seems embarrassed about his home background. He may generally try to prevent people from knowing about his economic status. He may refuse to accept assistance or gifts. Such a child may be unusually sensitive to the attitudes of other people; he may have a chip on his shoulder. We may find that a child tends to defend frequently his economic and family status. He may boast about his possessions or those of his family. On the other hand, we may find that he seems to have lost his self-respect. In this category we may also find children who tend to hoard a variety of useless objects.

We have emphasized insecurity as it relates to economic matters. The child who has developed this insecurity develops it in a social setting which continues to influence him. In other words, insecurity has already been produced and now the same influences aggravate it. In the home, parents sometimes discuss finances in the presence of the child in such a manner as to create an atmosphere of uncertainty about the future. The same sort of anxiety may be brought on in countless things parents may say and do to a child with regard to matters involving money and material possessions. In the school, economic insecurity may be further increased when collections are made in the classroom or when children are required to purchase costumes or equipment. As some parents do, teachers may communicate to children a feeling of economic insecurity in the ways in which they speak of the future.

What are the possible feelings of a child living in a setting which breeds a need for economic security and increases the need as time passes? Does he seem to feel insecurity and inferiority apparently not warranted by actual conditions? Perhaps he feels that Dad's job may not continue; that tomorrow is negatively uncertain. He may feel depressed by news items relating to socio-economic problems. Perhaps he remembers "better times." He may feel moody about present uncertainty, bitter about rich-poor issues. He may feel that some people have too much. Perhaps he feels "caught" by social class. This child may feel unsure about the probability of future education (or of college). He may feel unsure about his own employment, housing, etc., and frequently he may feel that society at large is responsible for his "predicament."

We must emphasize again that feelings of economic insecurity arise in children of all social levels. You may have children in your room from upper-middle class families whose parents talk a great deal about expenses, about the high cost of everything, about high taxes and inflation; and they may say dark things about the impending future. They little know that some of the things they say may have tremendous impact upon the emotional stability of their children. Do *not* think that this particular need is to be investigated only amongst children of the poor. Our researches show clearly that the feeling of economic insecurity can be present in the children of the very rich.

On the sheet which includes the names of all your children, enter in column three the frequency and the intensity with which the need for economic security is manifested by the kinds of behaviors described above. Do this only for the few children you plan to work with as "probable needs cases."

FREQUENCY	INTENSITY
1—every month or so	a—extremely mild symptoms
2—every few weeks	b—on the mild side
3—every week	c—mild toward severe
4—several times weekly	d—on the severe side
5—daily	e—serious disturbance
6—several times daily	f—extremely serious disturbance

IV. THE NEED FOR FREEDOM FROM FEAR

A child with many fears, with many anxieties, is a difficult child to teach. A fearful child is not a stable child and may be a bad though indirect influence on the conduct of the whole group. In this section we want to recognize those children who have irrational fears, fears of things they should not fear.

It is the chronic behavior of the child with many fears that we are interested in, those behaviors of a child which are more or less characteristic. Many fears are expressed verbally by children. In one way or another, they often express fear of persons in authority (policemen, the principal, teachers, doctors, etc.) and their father. A child may frequently express fear of death. He may say he is afraid he will die, or that his mother or father or teacher will die. Frequently a child of this type expresses concern about the need to be careful in sports and about illness. He may talk about the dangerous aspects of machines, automobiles, airplanes or vacuum cleaners. Often these children reveal in their conversation fear of insects, animals and the like: bugs in general, mice, cats, dogs, lions, tigers. Sometimes we hear a child say he's afraid of some other children, the more aggressive ones, or the older ones. Very often the child who has many fears tells us he's afraid of the dark, or thunder and lightning, wind, rain, storms or fire. Genuine fear of academic failure is frequently evident. This is the child who asks, "Will I pass?" He is afraid of getting "bad marks" in school, afraid to take home his report card. Fear of ridicule is not uncommon. A child may be terribly afraid of "what people say" about his clothing, his possessions, his parents' possessions, his home, his facial features, his speech, mannerisms, etc. He also may be very much afraid of what people will say about the fact that he is a member of a minority economic, social, religious or national group. Very often such children express fears of abstract phenomena: "ghosts," "spooks," bad men, the devil. These are the children who are likely to say, "The goblins will get us." They may also express fear of God. Such a child may be fearful of himself, sometimes running away from home, from school, or from the play-ground. He may be forever hiding. He may spend much time day-dreaming, worrying about what might happen.

Children so full of fear of so many things are apt to act nervous when they are about to take an examination, when they are asked to write in class or to take part in school plays. This nervous child also suffers physiological symptoms of fear when he is in the presence of more aggressive children and in the presence of adults in authority. When he sees someone injured or he sees blood, he may grow pale and tremble, get "sick" or faint. Redness of face, apparent tension, alternation between relaxation and tension, "inexplicable" weak-ness, nausea, inability to sleep, enuresis, fatigue, dizziness and in-voluntary excretion are not uncommon to such children. The child with a strong need to be free from fear may be an uncooperative child also. He may refuse to take part in the more active sports and activities; he may refuse to go to the school nurse or doctor; he may refuse to take part in school plays; he may "beg off" or say he doesn't know when called upon. This type of child generally refuses to try new things.

We have said that a fearful child is often an unstable child and may be a bad influence on the conduct of others. Let us turn now to some of the things adults may do that tend to increase the irrational fears in this child. We often hear people admonishing him to the effect that "the police will take care of you" or "if you do that you'll never go to heaven." "You'll turn out just like your Uncle John" or "You'll end up in the reform school" are frequent expressions. The scared child is very frequently threatened: "I'll put you in the closet if you're not good" or "If you don't get busy, you won't pass." Fear of injury is often aggravated by people who say to this child: "You might cut off your finger if you use that" or "You'll get hurt and have to go to the hospital." How often have we heard adults say to children, "Don't go near the dog; he will bite you" or "Don't touch that; it has germs on it" or "Be careful or you'll get infection in that sore." Sometimes fear is inculcated through inference, such as the occasions on which an adult may say to such a child: "Hurry inside! It's lightning" or "Don't go out there; it's dark." Among these children who are beset by fears are those who are burdened with more worries when a parent rather frequently tells him, "You'd be sorry if I died." "Be careful, you'll fall" and "Don't play with them; they're rough" are statements this type of child hears all too frequently.

It is in an environment where children see adults pulling shades when there is lightning, running away from harmless animals, and crying out when startled by insects, that irrational fears flourish in a child. Sometimes they see affectation in the behavior of their parents in the presence of "the boss," the principal or someone in another social class. Unnatural behavior in the presence of death, dwelling on catastrophies that have happened or might happen, refusal to go to the doctor because of fear, magnifying the extent of injuries, and frightening children about the phenomena of sex may be classified among the acts frequently indulged in by adults in the presence of children whose fears ought to be dispelled.

Is it possible for us to capture the feelings of a child possessed with fear? Do you think any of these statements express his feelings: He feels nervous most of the time; tired, nauseous when he is afraid; feels dizzy or paralyzed lots of times. He is afraid of policemen, the principal, teachers. He is afraid to recite in class. He dreads recounting some accident or dangerous experience. Often this child feels panicky, helpless, or he feels like running away. He may resent others for not really helping him allay his fears, and he may feel that strange things and new experiences are terrible threats to his security. Sometimes afraid to be thought of as a coward, he may be outwardly brash, noisy and presumably "unafraid" but inwardly quaking.

Such a child may frequently feel like hiding in his room with the pillow over his head; he may wish he could stop being afraid. Often he wishes very much that he could convince adults how terrifying some things are.

On the sheet which includes the names of all your children, enter in column four the frequency and the intensity with which the need for freedom from fear is manifested by the kinds of behaviors described above. Again do this only for those children you regard as "probable needs cases." Use the following scale:

FREQUENCY	INTENSITY
1—every month or so	a—extremely mild symptoms
2—every few weeks	b—on the mild side
3—every week	c—mild toward severe
4—several times weekly	d—on the severe side
5—daily	e—serious disturbance
6—several times daily	f—extremely serious disturbance

V. THE NEED FOR LOVE AND AFFECTION

Love, affection, and warmth in human relations seem to be the gift of almost every mother to her child in the earliest days of life. Emotional security, affection, intimacy, someone in whom to confide are wonderful possessions! To be deprived of them, to feel unloved, to have no one to like intensely are terribly severe deprivations. In this section, we are looking for children who seem to be unloved, those not receiving their human share of human warmth.

With the elementary school child this need for love and affection is almost exclusively a family matter. The warmth and affection is family-shared. The relationships to Mother and Dad, sisters and brothers supply the need in many, many cases.

The need for love and affection is often indicated in things a child may say. Often such a child may openly express a desire for demonstrations of affection, as when he says he wishes his mother or father would love him more, or that he wishes his parents liked him as much now as they did when he was younger. In his relationships with his teacher, he may frequently express a desire to sit next to her, or he may say: "You don't love me any more" or "Do you like me best?" or "You do love me, don't you?" It is not uncommon to hear a child exclaim, "You hate me!" A desire for more attention is often expressed by a child with a strong need for love and affection, as when he may say that he wishes he could talk things over with his parents more often or that he wishes his parents would take more interest in him or pay more attention to him. Such a child may also say that he wishes his parents would play with him more often or he wishes his parents were not too busy to talk to him. On the other hand, a child with a need for love and affection may express a desire to demonstrate his affection when he says he wishes he had someone he liked very much, or that he could do things that would show his parents how much he really likes them. This child may also have a tendency to continually ask his teacher personal questions.

A child with a need for love and affection often seems to be obviously demanding demonstrations of affection. He may make frequent requests to hold his teacher's hand, or to sit on teacher's lap and be fondled. This child may generally display a desire to snuggle up to people, or to put his head on his teacher's lap. Some of these children may indulge in "flight reactions" such as running away from home. Some may be truant or delinquent, or lie frequently. A child who is lacking in love and affection may shower affection on others. He may have violent "crushes" on members of the same or opposite sex, or he may show unusual displays of affection toward animals, dolls and toys. The girl who specializes in baby-sitting may be among the children with this need. Often we find that such a child is a "lackey" for his loved one. Frequently he clings to his mother or some familiar adult, and he may not venture out alone even if old enough to do so. His demeanor may be generally characterized by other actions. He may be very sensitive and his feelings may be easily hurt, especially when criticism comes from his loved one. He may be generally apathetic and listless. He may cry easily. He may suck his finger or he may over-eat. He may get sick frequently. Often a child with a need for love and affection demonstrates great interest in love stories. He may be a "bookworm"; he may be an avid reader of such stories, or be especially fond of "romance" in the movies or on the radio and T.V.

When we say to such a child, "Don't come to me with your troubles" or "If you can't fight your own battles don't come to me," we are likely to intensify his need. We may do this, too, when we say to this child, "I can't give you all of my time" and "I don't like boys like that" or "Why do you cry so much?" When we display no interest in the child or his work, when we disregard his need for physical love and attention, when we are too busy to talk things over with him or when we create a situation of sibling rivalry, we may aggravate his feelings of being unwanted, rejected. Though we cannot be sure, it may be that such a child feels as though no one loves him. He may want above all else to be hugged and kissed and fondled. He may be very angry at his parents. He may "hate" or be jealous of his younger brother or sister, or he may have those feelings about his stepfather or stepmother. Frequently, such a child may wish that his father had a job that wouldn't keep him away from home so much. Perhaps he feels like running away from home. He may wish fervently that he would get sick and die. He may love his puppy or kitten or doll very much. He may "love" to eat, especially sweets. He may love his teacher or some other adult very much. Feeling generally insecure and depressed, he may frequently feel like crying. Perhaps he wishes his teacher would pay attention to him instead of doing something else. He may feel a strong compulsion to pick up and read every love story magazine he sees. Perhaps this child is very much in love with a boy or girl in school, or he may fondly remember how he felt when an aunt or uncle or other adult fondled or hugged him. Often such a child wishes there were more love stories in the movies. It is very likely that above all, he wants to be loved and he wants to love someone.

On your class sheet which includes the names of all your children, enter in column five the frequency and intensity with which the need for love and affection is manifested by the kinds of behaviors described above. Use the following scale, and do it only for the special cases you have in mind.

FREQUENCY	INTENSITY
1—every month or so	a—extremely mild symptoms
2—every few weeks	b—on the mild side
3—every week	c—mild toward severe
4—several times weekly	d—on the severe side
5—daily	e—serious disturbance
6—several times daily	f—extremely serious disturbance

VI. THE NEED TO BE FREE FROM INTENSE FEELINGS OF GUILT

The process of growing up is also the process of making mistakes. Some children have such abnormally high standards for themselves that they have a sense of guilt with respect to much of their achievement. Sometimes adults set standards for children which are altogether too high, with the result that the child develops deep feelings of guilt. To be overwhelmed with deep feelings of guilt means a debasing of ourselves. Under those circumstances we feel "small," inadequate, incompetent or dishonest, and we think the eyes of the world are focused on us. To feel guilty is to feel "not clean inside." To feel guilty is to feel that one doesn't belong. We are looking for children who have feelings of this kind because we want to help them. In this section, let us concentrate on the symptoms of guilt as these symptoms show up in our classrooms.

Children who have a need to be free from feelings of guilt are likely to show this in things they say. Such a child may express guilt feelings about his relationships with people. He may say he wishes he hadn't lied to his mother or teacher, or that he wishes he wouldn't look down on people who are poor and uneducated, or that he wishes he had never made fun of other people. Frequently we may hear him say he wishes he didn't fight so much with other children or that he wishes he liked Negro children as well as white children. Often such a child may say he wishes his parents didn't expect him to be so obedient. It is not uncommon to hear this child express guilt feelings about his own actions, such as when he says he wishes he hadn't done something wrong, or he wishes he had never told naughty stories or said bad words. Frequently he may say he wishes he had never cheated or that he had been more obedient or he wishes he had never lost his temper.

Sometimes a child may reveal a need to be free from intense feelings of guilt by trying to avoid his teacher and others in authority, by "picking on himself," or by blaming himself for real or imaginary inferiorities. He may be extremely submissive. He may isolate himself and worry unduly over minor mistakes. He may blush easily or cry frequently. Often such a child shows signs of fearfulness, anxiety or indecision. He may be hyperconscientious. He may be shy, ill at ease around others, self-conscious, or he may cling to mother and father. Such a child may be described as pious, self-forgetful and placid. He may wash his hands unnecessarily many times and demand constant reassurance that he is behaving correctly or doing work correctly. This child may reveal feelings of guilt by his strong, overly-aggressive actions. He may be a poor loser and commit other such "offenses." Some children may reveal feelings of guilt by carrying on "campaigns," espousing "great causes" or "doing good for others." Sometimes a child may tell stories about "a friend of his" who committed some kind of an offense, while it is really an episode out of his own life.

Some children are ridiculed and nagged entirely too much. Sometimes public examples are made of a child who has done something that an adult of the group doesn't like. Moral codes are used to judge a child's conduct even when he might be ignorant of the code. Hasty judgments can be very damaging to the emotional security of children, as when we might say to a child, "No one ever did that in this class before" or "You're a very naughty child." When we say to a child, "Never say that again!" or "What if your mother knew that?" or "I never expected that of you," we may be intensifying his need to be free from guilt. Constantly throwing out remarks like "See how nicely the other children behave?" "What will the neighbors think?" "Remember God can see you," "You ought to have known better," "You have to be reminded too many times," "Shame on you!" "Everyone will have to suffer because of your actions," and "I'll tell your Dad on you" may have similar effects on the child who needs to be freed from intense feelings of guilt.

Sometimes we adults intensify feelings of guilt when we keep reminding children of their mistakes, when we act as though we always do the right thing, and when we scold children for actions and words they have copied from adults. When we don't allow a child to fully explain how he feels about things, the child may have one

motive while we suspect another. Guilt feelings in a child are probably increased when we continue to judge his acts by our adult standards and expectations, when we show expressions of "shock," when
we make him apologize, and when we are constantly nagging.

What kinds of feelings are engendered in these ways, and what
feelings may there be underlying the behavior of a child who has a
need to be free from intense feelings of guilt? Perhaps he feels
ashamed of himself, disloyal, dishonorable. Perhaps he feels that he
is unique in his faults and feels little or no respect for himself. Frequently such a child may feel embarrassed, small, ashamed of his
dreams. Perhaps he is always running himself down, thinking that he
is always doing something wrong. Is it possible that he feels he must
always be on top in competition, or that he feels ashamed of some
bad plays he has made in games? Perhaps this child just generally
feels guilty about the trouble he thinks he creates.

On your class sheet which includes the names of all your children,
enter in column six the frequency and intensity with which the need
to be free from intense feelings of guilt is manifested by the kinds of
behaviors described above. Use the following scale and record your
judgments of only those children who seem to be "needs cases."

FREQUENCY	INTENSITY
1—every month or so	a—extremely mild symptoms
2—every few weeks	b—on the mild side
3—every week	c—mild toward severe
4—several times weekly	d—on the severe side
5—daily	e—serious disturbance
6—several times daily	f—extremely serious disturbance

VII. THE NEED FOR SHARING AND SELF-RESPECT

There are many pressures on the growing child to conform to what
adults prefer. The process of growing up is ordinarily accompanied
by thousands of "don'ts" uttered by older persons in the immediate
environment. Some children come to feel that they have practically
no liberty in deciding things for themselves. They are told what to
do, when to do it, where to do it and when to stop doing it. Frustration may come from feeling pushed around too much. Our attention
is now directed toward identifying children who may feel that everybody is trying to run their lives, who feel that they are not respected

as persons, who feel that the good life is not for them, and if it is, tl will have to wait for many years before they can enjoy it.

Sometimes such a child may express the desire to want other peo ple to have faith in his judgment, as when he says he wishes that his opinions were asked for more often or he wishes his teacher wanted him to take part in making the rules of the school. He may say he wishes adults didn't always take the words out of his mouth or he wishes others were interested in his ideas and questions. Frequently he may say that he wishes others did not try to do his planning for him or that his parents wanted his help in making plans and rules in the family, or that adults wouldn't place restrictions on speech which apply only to him. Ofttimes such a child reveals that he would like other people to cooperate with him better. He may insist on doing jobs for people, especially if he may work with someone on the job. We may frequently hear him say he wishes that other children didn't want their way so much or that other children and he could decide upon things together. Often he may express the wish that adults not always talk "over his head." We may also find that such a child frequently engages in boasting.

The child who needs to share may seem to be withdrawing into a shell. Such a child may often permit himself to be pushed aside so that another may have his place. He may play with children considerably younger than himself, or if rejected by the group he may withdraw completely. This child may act indifferent and apathetic toward group activities and members of the group; he may cry easily and whine and whimper a lot. On the other hand, a child with a strong need for sharing and self-respect may seem to be frequently rebellious or disobedient toward parents, brothers and sisters, grandparents, other relatives, teachers, friends and schoolmates. He may often try deception and bluffing. He may resent being pushed aside and he may fight back. Such a child may contradict people who are talking, especially when he has not been asked to share in the conversation or activity. He may continually pretend to be an authority on any subject under discussion, interrupting conversations to give information even though not asked for it. This is the child who "butts in" at any time; he imposes his leadership upon the group and may be very dictatorial. He may steal and generally disobey instructions.

When we say to a child, "You're too young" or "You're too little," we are probably enhancing his need for sharing and self-respect. Similar feelings may be aroused in the child when we say to him, "You don't use your head" or "Don't you know any better?" or

"Haven't you any sense?" or "Don't be silly." We may often say things such as "Be your age" or "Won't you ever grow up?" or "That's all wrong. This is the right way" or "Let me do that."

This child frequently finds himself forced into activities, the plans for which were made without considering him. Family vacations, financial plans, recreation, all of these affect him. Yet, one seldom gives him an opportunity to make decisions or suggestions. In school as well as at home, this child generally does not have an opportunity to do things. People stop talking when he enters the room; he is often belittled and frequently criticized as a person in front of the group.

When we take away a child's privileges, when we don't let a child share in plans and express his opinions, when we reject the work that a child has done rather than help him and let him make another effort, when we neglect allowing the slow, shy child to participate, and when we don't provide an opportunity for each child to share in room projects, we may be increasing the need for sharing and self-respect.

Would it be possible for us to guess how such a child feels? Perhaps he feels inadequate, as though he as a person is not respected. Perhaps he wants very much to have something to say about the propositions which affect him. This child may frequently want to help others in their activities and projects. He may possibly feel that everyone is suspicious of him or his ideas. Confused, bewildered, he may feel resentful or very much discouraged. Perhaps you suspect he wishes his parents would allow him more privacy and knock on the door before entering the room. A child who feels the need for sharing and self-respect may often feel there is a conspiracy against him or generally as though his ideas and opinions are not worthwhile.

On your class sheet which includes the names of all your children, enter in column seven the frequency and intensity with which the need for sharing and self-respect is manifested by the kinds of behaviors described above. Use the following scale and record only for those students who seem to be "needs cases."

FREQUENCY	INTENSITY
1—every month or so	a—extremely mild symptoms
2—every few weeks	b—on the mild side
3—every week	c—mild toward severe
4—several times weekly	d—on the severe side
5—daily	e—serious disturbance
6—several times daily	f—extremely serious disturbance

VIII. THE NEED FOR SELF-CONCEPT AND UNDERSTANDING

Some children seem bewildered by this world. They can't make much sense out of it. When we are bewildered, when we cannot make sense out of what is happening around us, our earth begins to shake a little. We are unsteady. We begin to entertain some doubt about our *selves.* We may believe that other people and other children are quite all right, but we are the ones who aren't what we should be. We believe that there are things we ought to know, because knowing them would give us some confidence in ourselves. *But, we don't know them.* And faith in our *selves* weakens. There are a number of children like this, and among children of minority groups the number is very high. Sometimes they don't know the questions to ask. At other times they ask and ask and never get adequate answers. Their questions sometimes are fearfully direct and relate to questions that are very controversial in nature. If the school day neglects these questions, if the answers given result in even greater confusion, if the child thinks he doesn't understand what's going on around him, he may become emotionally disturbed. Let's look at some of the symptoms that this type of child may reveal.

He may constantly ask questions about varied topics, demanding immediate answers; he may continually probe to discover details of things and situations. When he gets answers from parents and teachers, he may doubt their validity. Among the numerous queries he makes, he may say: He wishes he knew why we have so many wars when almost everyone says he wants peace; he wishes he knew what causes the trouble between Negroes and white people; he wishes he knew why people say that everyone is equal when some people have much more money than others; he wishes someone would help him find out the difference between what is right and what is wrong.

Frequently such a child reveals dissatisfaction with his understanding of things and situations. He may say, "They're trying to keep something from me," or he may ask, "Why do people hush me up when I ask about sex?" Perhaps this child says he wishes he knew how he could look out for himself and at the same time be fair to other people. Often we hear such a child say he wishes someone would help him make up his mind when he is uncertain about things or that he wishes so many people wouldn't mix him up in what he believes. Rather frequently such children may express their desire for more information. We may hear a child say he wishes he knew how he could like his own country best and at the same time like people in other countries too, or he wishes someone would help him to see what his purposes really are, or he wishes his parents would help him more to understand himself, or he wishes he could get help in learning to know what he should believe. Sometimes such children tell us they wish they could understand some of the big words they read.

Ofttimes a child who has a need for understanding will assume sole or special responsibility for securing information. He may accept the opinions of others without question; he may read constantly; he may be an "authority" on birds, fish, rocks, planes, guns and other specialities. Frequently such a child may become aggressive in seeking information. He may ask "why" repeatedly; he may continually question authority. He may be intolerant and prejudiced. This child may also continually take mechanical things apart. Often we find such children employing mature work habits. They may be discriminating, reading books above their age level on a wide variety of subjects and using the library frequently.

Often parents give these children the idea that *later* they will understand, that adults and teachers will explain the things that are confusing; but frequently these explanations are not forthcoming and the curriculum continues to be dull. It is not unusual to find adults saying to such a child: "You'll find out about that when you're older" or "I've explained it three times already." When he is continually rebuked by statements like "Tommy, you ask too many questions. Why don't you be quiet?" how might such a child feel? When we don't answer his questions so that he can understand, how does he feel?

This child feels confused, bewildered. There is so very much that he wants to know. People don't answer his questions adequately. Adults are stupid. School is "dumb," not interesting. He feels cheated when he doesn't get the answers he is seeking. He wants to understand the things that are confusing to him. He feels very much discouraged that people don't want to help him and thinks they are only trying to confuse him. Frequently, he feels that adults don't tell him the truth, that people are always trying to keep something from him; he feels rejected. He may often be afraid to ask questions. He resents adults who tell him he is "too young to understand." Often he is convinced it *is* an adult world mostly, and he can't understand why. He is bewildered at the differences between what adults say and what they do. He feels even more curious about something when he gets an evasive answer; he feels very good when he has the answers to important questions.

On your class sheet which includes the names of all your children, enter in column eight the frequency and the intensity with which the

need for understanding is manifested by the kinds of behaviors described above. Use the following scale and keep track only for those
children who seem to be "needs cases."

FREQUENCY	INTENSITY
1—every month or so	a—extremely mild symptoms
2—every few weeks	b—on the mild side
3—every week	c—mild toward severe
4—several times weekly	d—on the severe side
5—daily	e—serious disturbance
6—several times daily	f—extremely serious disturbance

5

DOS & DON'TS
OF THE
NEEDS THEORY

Current educational theory suggests that when emotional needs are frustrated, children are apt to find it much more difficult to learn. Since serious behavior problems are often caused by frustration, it seems to follow that teachers must learn how to identify some of the more important emotional needs of the children in their classrooms. In the foregoing pages the attempt was made to explain the needs theory and to indicate ways of identifying some of the emotional needs of children.

Identifying is not enough. We do need to be able to recognize behavior that suggests the presence of needs, but we also have to know what to do about it. Teachers want help in working with children whose needs are not being adequately met. This book was written for that purpose. It is intended as a source book of suggestions, a tentative guide to action, and I hope it will be helpful to the thousands of teachers, sincere, hard-working people, who are trying to meet the needs of their students.

Through the ordinary processes of child-rearing we come to cherish highly certain kinds of consideration from other people. We learn to prize love and affection; we learn to want praise, recognition and feelings of accomplishment; we learn to want to be relatively free from intense feelings of guilt and of fear; we learn to want friends and to be friends. The process of growing up brings with it the acceptance of many of these values of the culture in which we live. We have learned to want certain qualities in our human relationships. When these are denied to us, we say that certain needs are being thwarted. When these needs remain unsatisfied, our theory suggests that some of us become *aggressive* toward others or toward property. Some of us vent our aggression inwardly: We punish ourselves by becoming victims of one or more of a great variety of psychosomatic disturbances. Some of us become unusually submissive, shy, or meek; some of us tend to withdraw from social situations which present a threat to us—we decide not to participate—and some of us regress to earlier stages of development.

These frustrated needs of ours also reveal themselves in our daily behavior in more subtle ways. In the previous pages we have described the behaviors which seem symptomatic of some of the more important needs. In this volume we present a large number of suggestions for teachers on ways of working with children who seem to have these symptoms.

An extension of the theory suggests that if we could identify some of the more important needs of children and develop ways of meeting those needs, then the behavior of children would change, learning would become easier, and the quality of personal and of associated living would improve: There would be better human relations. This description of the theory certainly over-simplifies human behavior as we know it. A child never seems to be all of one thing and nothing of another. These "human needs" do not come in atomistic packages. My own experience testifies that there is much overlapping. Many children seem to have more than one need, and we must address ourselves to ever-growing and ever-changing children. Nevertheless, we can identify major trends in behavior, and we can emphasize certain things as we work with individual children and groups of children.

We have concentrated our attention on *eight* emotional needs, their symptoms in behavior, and what might help to alleviate their frustrations. *We do believe that there are many other needs of children.* We do think, however, that the eight needs preoccupying our attention are of unusually great importance to classroom teachers. If we can help to meet these needs, we shall be in a better position to prepare ourselves for meeting still others. Several pieces of doctoral research have been conducted in order to test the theory in practice. At the moment our educational experiments suffer from inadequate controls, and it is practically impossible to draw definite conclusions from the evidence that we collect. However, all of the experiments to date tend to support this theory: As teachers try to meet the emotional needs of children, learning tends to improve as measured by scores on standardized tests; social acceptance tends to increase; extreme forms of aggression tend to decrease; the frequency of on-set and the intensity of certain physical symptoms seem to decline and school attendance improves. Given this much basis in experience, it seems worthwhile to continue efforts to experiment with different groups in many different places.

Teachers are warned to proceed carefully and cautiously in their planning. It is very easy to fall into some critical situations. If you decide to work with one or two children as a "starter," try to foresee some of the possible consequences of your own changed behavior. If you have been unusually strict with a youngster and you suddenly change by letting him express some of the symptoms of a frustrated need—that is, if you quite suddenly become more permissive—you must not be surprised if the child's behavior is on the aggressive side. Then when that happens, if you suddenly shift back again, you may actually be intensifying his needs. It becomes impossible *for him* to understand you and your inconsistent behavior. In other words, consistency of behavior on the part of the teacher is probably of very great importance to the children. You will probably not be successful in meeting needs unless you carry out a determined and consistent program day after day, week after week. We all have moments when we slip back a step, but if we have our eye on the goal and are determined to meet needs, and if we master some of the techniques, we are pretty sure to make substantial headway.

If you try to meet some of the emotional needs of a few children, what will happen to the other children? This question is often asked, and in the actual situation, surprisingly enough, it seems to have little relevance. Just as you now often pay attention to a single child, in trying to meet the emotional needs of a particular child, you will be doing the same so far as attention is concerned.

Is it your job to meet the emotional needs of the children in your room? The answer is no. You really have no more responsibility in this matter than the personnel of other social institutions, and much less responsibility than parents. In fact, your primary job is to promote learning. Now, if something gets in the way of learning, including how to get along with others, quite obviously you have a responsibility to do something about it. If the vision of a particular child is suspected as a cause, you try to do something about it. If his hearing is bad, you do something about that. In the same way, if frustrated needs seem to be blocking the learning process, you will want to do something about it, and this volume may be of help to you.

Are you expected to be a clinical psychologist or analyst or psychiatrist? By all means, NO! You will do the things that can normally be expected of teachers in group situations and in the typical teacher-child or teacher-parent interview. If you have any reason to suspect that a child has some very deep psychological problems, you do have a responsibility to take the matter up with your school officials. This volume contains only those things that can normally be expected of teachers in rather typical classroom situations.

One last qualification: I have listed eight needs; I have described their behavioral symptoms, and in the pages which follow I am going to recommend things to do and things to avoid in trying to meet these needs. Remember, however, that I have said that these needs overlap, that they often come together, and that there is no rigorous proof of the existence of any one of them independent of other needs. I also want to emphasize that these suggestions are not regarded as specific cures for a specific cause. The suggestions are submitted to you as tentative guides to action. Don't take them as blueprints. You will think of many additional things, and depending upon your local situation and the particular child under consideration, you will do what seems appropriate to you.

As you try to meet the needs of a particular child, you may find it somewhat difficult to change some of the patterns of *your own behavior.* Here are some suggestions that other teachers have found useful.

1. Convince yourself over and over again that your job is not to hide symptoms, not to ignore behaviors, but to find out *the causes* of unsocial behavior. If you become convinced of this point of view, you are more likely to give a child a chance to express his symptoms, thus giving you a larger chance to understand him.

2. From time to time reassure yourself that the most important thing in any child's life is his own thought, growth and development. He isn't nearly as much concerned as you and I are about his status in academic affairs. He is inwardly disturbed and he wants to straighten himself out. He wants to be happy and he wants to be creative and independent, and these unmet needs are getting in the way.

3. Sometimes teachers recognize in themselves a tendency to be somewhat biased toward one or two children. If you have such a bias,

try to bring it to the level of consciousness and recognize it in your-self. When you do, there is more of a chance that you might compen-sate for it. There is more of a chance that you will be likely to give that child "a better break."

4.   Some teachers have found it helpful when they are very much disturbed to leave the room for a moment. They come back a bit more calm, poised, stable and more ready to meet the situation. Teachers sometimes ask a child to take a message to another teacher and thus are free for a moment or two from the pressure which this particular child exerts in a classroom.

5.   Some teachers have found it helpful to recognize within them-selves a developing emotion as their relationships with the child become tense. These teachers sometimes say to a child, "I seem to be getting excited about this. Are you getting excited too?" or they sometimes say, "For some reason or another I seem to be disturbed. Can you understand why I am?" or they say, "I think I could be happier if we talked about this later."

6.   As your point of view tends toward that of trying to meet needs, you will probably overlook many things that up to this moment you really may have paid too much attention to. Where one does quite a lot of criticizing or fault finding, a child is apt to feel nagged. He comes to feel that he is being picked on, that someone is unfair to him. In working with these unusually disturbed children, it is a good idea to plan to overlook certain things and not to consider everything equally important.

7.   It takes as long to be mean to a child as it does to be pleasant, and we must be sure not to waste our precious time if we want children to be more secure.

I. MEETING THE NEED FOR BELONGING

In order to feel good about his life every child has to have some sense of belonging. He needs to find people he likes and wants to be with. Moreover, he needs to find among his age-mates children who like him and who want him. He wants to be a part of group work, and he wants to be thought of when people he knows are deciding to do something together. If he is absent from school, he would like to feel that he is missed, and that the group isn't what it would be if he were there. Every child seems to like occasions when other children want him to join them. He is pleased when they choose him for a committee, want him on their team, ask him to go along to the movies or on a hike. Children feel left out when these things seem to be happening to their friends and they themselves are not invited. This is equally true of parties that are given in neighborhood homes. It is true also inside the pattern of family life: Where there is a feeling of belonging, where children feel that they are wanted, even needed, they have a sense of rapport, a sense of identification with the group, and this is a feeling that increases inner security.

The feeling of being left out culminates sometimes in a great feeling of insecurity in the child. His world is threatened. Normally, the child with a need for belonging is often in a state of tension. He desires above everything else to relax and to be one with the others. Over all there is a feeling of helplessness, a feeling of insecurity, a feeling of decreased personal worth, a feeling that whereas the other children are quite all right, he himself must in some strange way be different because he is not being accepted. There are many things that people do to children which make them feel unwanted, make them feel as if they do not belong to the group or the class or the club. There are also many things that people do which make children feel that they are wanted, are an integral part of the group, really belong.

Here are some suggestions, not a blueprint, which may indicate things to do and things not to do in an effort to pay attention to that "internal crying" of children whose emotional needs are thwarted and who feel unwanted or rejected.

Some Things to Do

If a child is absent for a day or two from school, let him or his parents or his brothers and sisters know that you realize that he has been away. Sometimes it is possible to telephone or to talk with a relative and to mention that you have missed him and that you hope he will be back soon. Sometimes children in the room will take the responsibility for getting in touch with the family and make reports. Sometimes a rather long strip of wrapping paper or wall paper is used, and every child in the room writes some message on it, and the whole thing is sent home or to the hospital. When the child returns to school, be sure to make some little mention of it. Welcome him back and indicate that you are glad he is back and that you missed him while he was gone. Some mention of his absence might be made at times before the whole group. If, upon his return, he needs some particular program for "catching up" on his absence, it is helpful to take children into the planning and make it an occasion for other children to have the chance of helping him and being with him.

Your own friendliness toward all children will be a factor in the situation with these particular children whom you are trying to help. Perhaps you can say a word of welcome to the class if it is a departmentalized situation. When children come in in the morning, you might set up a situation in which you say good morning to each of them. When it comes time to go home in the afternoon, you might be able to arrange a situation in which you say good night to them individually or as a group. With respect to the individual children whom you are especially trying to help, it will pay dividends to make these good mornings and good nights warm, personal affairs. Sometimes you realize that a particular child would welcome more intimate contact with you, not just for the contact of course. Everything that we do should be in the direction of making him feel happier in the personal relationship. Therefore, for some children you might schedule meetings after school when you could talk with them in more informal situations. The talks could be freer and perhaps more intimate. You could have experiences that you might share with each other. On some occasions you will make it a point to have lunch with these individuals.

Walk to the corner or walk to the bus with a child after school. Sometimes it is best to spend part of a recess period with a child. Perhaps it is possible to become greatly interested in his extra-curricular activities. Try to find out what he is doing outside of school and become concerned about his success in these things. Sometimes it is best to invite the child to go to a movie, or to a concert, or to a school picnic, or to a family outing. Sometimes it is possible to arrange for the celebration of children's birthdays in a classroom. Be particularly sure that these individual children are given that recognition! The singing of happy birthday, the eating of a few cookies, or some other recognition of the fact that an anniversary has arrived is important. These parties and get-togethers often help the child to get started in some kind of participation.

Be on the lookout for unmet needs of belonging with respect to new children who come to the neighborhood. Perhaps you can appoint a "big brother" or "big sister" who will orient the newcomer to the school, introduce him to many children, and help to make him feel at home. Help the new child to understand some of the rules in the school and the degree of permissiveness that is acceptable. By taking the child into consideration on many occasions you can help him to see that you want him to belong to the class and you want the class to belong to him. During the first weeks that a newcomer is in your school, be sure to talk with him often about any problems that he may have or any difficulties that he is experiencing.

Sometimes you may encourage changes in seating allowing the children to make their choices and developing a plan that best meets those selections. Sometimes the elected officers are rotated every two weeks or every four weeks so that every person has an opportunity to be on different committees and to be an officer of a committee. Where you assign responsibilities or honors, these too can be rotated, and under these circumstances children have a greater feeling of belonging because all of them are sharing in the rewards.

Sometimes children have difficulty in belonging because they are deficient in skills. Try to find out other strengths of these children. Do some intensive remedial work at times and also bring in a recognition of things that are done outside of school. Sometimes it is possible to mention something about appearance, or clothing, or ornaments, or belongings. A child appreciates these comments just as much as an adult. If we are alert, we can find things to be cheerful about and to comment upon favorably.

Sometimes we teachers ask children what they are going to be "when they grow up." This would show an interest even though it is remote. What probably is even better is to inquire about their present purpose: things they want to learn, things they want to do, things they have done. Children want attention paid to them as they are *now*. Their present lives are very important to them and they would like to talk about them. As you develop an atmosphere in which their concerns are given importance, they come to feel as though they belong. In the same way, children come to feel that they belong if they have some freedom of movement in the room, if the so-called discipline requirements are not too strict. They come to feel that they belong if they can share in making some of the rules. Moreover, if they help to make the rules, the rules can be quoted back to them and they see some sense in the situation. The same children might resent some individual always telling them what to do and what not to do.

This is an important point: When you criticize or find some fault, try to remove criticism from the child as a person and direct your criticism to some particular thing he wrote, or he said, or he did. Give advice on a particular happening; otherwise you may leave the impression that you dislike or have less respect for him as a person. If you understand how he differs from other children, you will be able to accept the things that he does because you know that they grow out of his experiences. Other children will be different because they have had other experiences. You will tolerate other experiences because you know children come from different kinds of homes and from different cultural backgrounds. On many occasions, you will be pleased with differences, and you will help children to see that these differences make the class richer and more varied and hence more valuable as a group. If you have a particular criticism to make, try with all your heart not to make it public. Try to see a child individually; try to speak to him privately or try to arrange a time when you can.

Some Things Not to Do

Don't be casual about absences of children who have unmet emotional needs. Don't overlook their feelings about being out of things. Don't take for granted that they are supposed to be in school, like all the rest of the children, and therefore neglect to welcome them back. Don't think of them as completely integrated people who do not need these little words of reassurance that. make us all feel so good even when our needs are fairly well met. Don't forget about them when they are away.

It is best for you not to project on children some of your own unmet needs. Take stock of yourself. As a rule, do you tend to be on the friendly side, to be a cheerful sort of person to live with? Don't grumble and crab about the group as a group, or about the way some individuals in it tend to spoil the record in the group. Especially for these individual children, don't try to avoid them; don't brush off their efforts to make contact with you. Don't neglect their ideas, and don't be too obvious in pushing one of these children away from you so that you can talk more readily with another child.

We can be indifferent to birthdays; we can be unfriendly in many relationships, and we do so at our peril! Don't neglect the warmth and friendliness that are required in a classroom. Don't have a room in which it is all work and no play, all seriousness and no fun, all strictness and no relaxation. Don't set yourself off too far from the children. Don't neglect to associate with them occasionally in many different ways. They get to know you in these situations and you get to know them better.

Don't take for granted that a new child will find his place and that that is his responsibility. Don't feel that a child can orient himself to a whole new neighborhood. Don't think that your sole job is an academic one and that if he meets the subject matter requirements of the grade that all is well. Don't push him out in front too often at the beginning. Take an interest in him but do it cautiously.

Don't set up a pattern that allows favoritism to show itself. Don't have a few children doing all the work. Don't let an election system get going that restricts the opportunities of many children to share in the work of the group. Don't let lack of ability restrict you from giving the children a chance to learn. Don't keep the children from mixing with others by some kind of fixed seating arrangements. Don't have them walk out of the classroom in a certain rigid, fixed way.

A child who isn't thought of, who seems to pass unnoticed in your presence, grows to be a little uncomfortable in your presence. He may want to have you notice that he is different today from what he was yesterday. If he has something new or different, he is pleased when you make mention of it. Don't overlook new appearances, new belongings, new activities, new hair-dos, new dresses, new ribbons, new shoes, unless it is pretty obvious that mention of them would be in bad taste or out of place.

Children learn through trying things and making mistakes, just as you and I do. Don't try to make the schoolroom situation a place in which everything is cut and dried. Don't exclude the children from discussions of policy and don't try to have the last word on everything. Because they are small or young, don't make the mistake of thinking that they are not important or that the feeling of importance for them is a trivial thing. They love to feel that they are part of things that are going on.

Be careful not to single out a child as the only one who hasn't followed the rules, or who has spoiled the record of absences or tardiness, or who is the only noisy one. Don't laugh at the mistakes of children and don't ridicule or embarrass them. Don't send a child out of the room for punishment unless it is for an unusually extreme kind of situation. Don't have him stand in a corner. Don't send him to the cloakroom. Don't have him sit with a girl, and don't isolate him from the others. Whatever you do, don't mistrust him before the group. Don't ever tell other children or other teachers something that a child has told you in confidence. Don't ever overlook his need for belonging.

Summary

So far we have presented many, many suggestions of things to do and things not to do if you are going to build within a child a feeling of belongingness. Each one of these activities by itself is quite meaningless. Even many of them taken together can be meaningless. What you do has to be brought into a relationship that makes for warm acceptance. What you do has to be done in a kindly, friendly, accepting manner. To try to do any of these things mechanically or automatically will probably result in no change. Your efforts should always be to promote a feeling of belonging and these are the ways that you choose to do it, but your own manner and the manner of children will, in large measure, determine the outcome. These activities must somehow or other be in an envelope of warm friendliness and trust and mutual confidence. Once you have that point of view, you will see many additional things to do and many other things to avoid if you are going to promote inner emotional security.

II. MEETING THE NEED FOR ACHIEVEMENT

The need for achievement develops in the early relationships between an infant and his mother. We can see how in the early months of his life the growing child receives an enormous amount of recognition, praise and reward. When a child has developed some feeling of personal worth, some sense of recognition, some sense of achievement, he adds measurably to his feeling of inner security. This is the way to start out the healthy growth and development of a child. I want to emphasize the fact that children need to have this feeling of accomplishment *throughout all their lives,* for when this need is frustrated the children's behavior becomes markedly different. All of us need praise, attention, and a feeling of independence. If we don't get it, we tend to feel inadequate and sometimes inferior. There is a real sense in which "love alone isn't enough." The child may feel that he is liked, but he wants also to be respected.

The feeling of worth each of us has, if we are to become sure of ourselves, must be proved again and again by achieving. In the most simple or difficult ways we are driven to prove our worth. The child with the need for achievement feels inadequate and inferior. He tends to be discouraged and depressed and will sometimes feel that there is no need even to attempt to achieve. Cut off from the praise of his associates and elders, he may feel hatred for the other children and may pick fights or quarrels with them. At other times, weighted down with his shortcomings, he will want only to be left alone, to brood and pity himself. Often he is quiet and submissive, allowing himself to be tossed one way or another by the day's events, feeling that whatever happens makes little difference to anyone around him. The child who feels that he is never given a chance to prove himself with something he can do well may wonder why it is that people seem never to be satisfied, no matter how hard he tries. He feels that he is an outsider, with no one interested enough to take time to teach him or to help him when he needs help. The world is "out of joint" to such a child, and he needs help.

What can we do to help meet his need for a feeling of achievement?

Some Things to Do

We can surely see to it that a child does not have frequent failure experiences. Once we sense that the standard we have set for him is too high, we can change the standard, select new assignments, plan new experiences with him that will give him feelings of success. We can let him set his own standard of speed and help him to see when that standard is improving. We can be sure to recognize times when he is successful, when he is made "blue," and when he has met his own standards.

Some children who have a need for achievement tend to make many excuses for their poor showing. Whatever you do, listen to these things carefully: Don't comment on every one of them. Accept his excuses as a kind of symptom that he is not feeling a sense of achievement. This is also true of boasting behavior. Listen to the boasting, but arrange for activities in which this child can have a solid sense of accomplishment. This is also true of lying, falsehoods, and cheating. These children often lie, cheat, or steal to increase their own sense of achievement, to get comments, and *to get the praise they want.* It is quite obvious that if they had received more attention, if they had been feeling a sense of accomplishment and of personal worth, they might not have indulged in these behaviors.

We need to be careful in giving rewards, and in general we need to place more emphasis on the *process* by which excellent accomplishment is made. If a child has a perfect spelling paper, instead of merely marking it 100, we can ask him what reasons he can give for his excellence. Then we can write those reasons on his paper, and we can reward him for his study habits, and his diligence, and other factors he might mention. We can be sure that the rewards are distributed widely among all children in the classroom. We shouldn't believe that it is justice to give rewards for only identical work. We can be sure to reward for effort, and to reward for steps along the way, and to reward for improvement over yesterday's efforts.

Make the assumption that a child *wants to learn* some things and try to find out what those things are. Make the assumption that he *wants to make efforts* but that he might be blocked. Make the assumption that he has the capacity for development and that you want to help him. Assume always that if you two understand each other, you can build a foundation that will develop into something bigger and better.

If the school is only a reading-and-writing school, there will be many children who will not be able to reveal their unusual talents. A schoolroom that has crayons and paint, wood and clay, textiles and cloth, hammers and nails and saws and wood, leather and large paper in abundance will offer to many children opportunities that the book-ish school does not allow. Where there is a variety of media to work in, many more children reveal diverse talents.

Children want to be skillful and competent in some things. Some-times the things they want skill in are of little concern to the teach-ers. If the teacher puts herself out a little bit to see that the child gets help in developing the skill that he thinks is important, she can give that child a sense of achievement. His concern might be with swim-ming or with other athletics, public speaking, musical ability, embroi-dery, sewing, or some aspect of the fine arts. The sensitive teacher will try to discover some of these wanted skills and will try to find some "experts" to whom the child might go for help. These experts might be other children, other teachers, parents in the neighbor-hood, or lay citizens. Hence, when a teacher pays attention to these concerns of children, she is helping to build a sense of achievement and independence.

Sometimes children get a sense of achievement when they are asked to help somebody else, and this is true of helping the teacher. They derive much satisfaction from being asked to help much younger children with more simple things.

Children can learn a lot from each other. Sometimes our schools are places where children are expected to report what they learned at home or what they studied last night. We teachers can work with children in such a way as to help them see that the school is a place to learn, that it is a place to learn from other people and from certain activities. Make it possible for children to get help from each other. Make it easy for them to tell what they do not know, and what they cannot do, and where they need help. When they start out on a job, make sure that they have some preparation for it and have some ideas about how to go about it. A good start is often half the job. As a child is helped to see more clearly what he is doing and what he is trying to do, it will be easier for him to make solid accomplish-ments. This will give him a feeling of achievement.

Occasionally children embark joyfully upon jobs and are greatly disappointed when they do not succeed. Sometimes we can help children to anticipate the possibilities of failure. We can help them see that failure itself is a solid learning and that the same mistake will probably not be repeated. Children learn under these circumstances that the teacher is realistic and not a perfectionist. They see that mistakes made are an asset because they show us what to avoid in the future. This is a planned process, and, as teachers engage in more of it with children, there will probably be a greater sense of achievement on the part of the children and a greater understanding of why failures take place. Under this circumstance, failure becomes a part of achievement.

We all know that children are at different developmental levels. Some children are ready to read and others are not. Some are ready for gang and group activities and others aren't. Some are ready for co-educational activities and some aren't. Some have voices that are "breaking," while others have matured to the place where this is in the past. A sense of achievement comes when tasks are well spaced and placed. Children have a sense of what they can do and what they would like to try to do. We should try to pace these activities to the tempo of the children and have their own ambitions guide the next steps.

To give children a sense of accomplishment, we should every once in a while provide an opportunity for them to summarize the work of several days or of several hours. We should ask them to tell what they have gained from their activities, and write their responses on the board. Sometimes children can write a letter to their parents to tell about these achievements. In this way, we show them that we are sensitive to their needs for achievement. Moreover, we are giving them a chance to tell what they have or have not learned and, if we listen carefully, we can make changes that will give them an even greater sense of achievement.

Our praise of what children do should always be sincere. We should not be praising them for things that do not merit praise. We must be sensitive to the idea of change, to evidence of effort, to intensity of purpose. We must be sure that when we give a reward, it has been earned, and we can arrange tasks for every child to help him merit such praise. Our reward should be sincere. Our encouragement should be on a sound basis. Our praise should be for what the child really has done or has tried to do.

Many children do things in our presence that are not up to our standards or to their own. Sometimes children notice differences themselves and see it *before* we do. Sometimes a single comment from us helps them to beware of something that they have done. This awareness is in itself, in most instances, sufficient motivation for learning. This consciousness on their part of what is wrong with the situation sets in motion a chain of ideas about what should be done.

Some Things Not to Do

We can surely see to it that there is NOT one standard for all the children in the class. We can avoid expecting the same quality of work, the same return of product from all children. We should also be careful of immediately setting new standards for the child who shows some progress, but rather let him rejoice for a while in the success of his achievement.

There is a danger in having such rewards as stars, candy, high marks, because these things come to be false symbols and often create a hostile kind of competition. We should try to explain that it is the effort, the planning, the persistence that is bringing rewards.

Be careful to avoid saying to a child that he isn't trying, he doesn't want to do things, he isn't interested, or he is unconcerned about what is going on. If he is really having difficulty, he is already feeling bad about it, and for you to say these things makes him angry when he feels that he has been trying. It is more beneficial to try to find out what he has been doing and trying to do.

Don't set tasks that always tax the maximum powers of a child, giving him a sense of struggle that always brings on tenseness. Be sure that he has a chance to do some of the things that are easier for him. Don't overlook the need each child has to show off a little bit. Each child wants to have some sense that he, too, has learned and made progress, and he wants to demonstrate his achievements.

When children lie, cheat, boast, or make excuses, be very sure that you do not argue with them in front of the class, and don't even argue with them in private interviews when they make excuses. Don't try to make them admit that they have done something that is wrong. Don't try to show that the boasting is ideal and vain. If you do, you are paying too much attention to symptoms, and not enough attention to those things that cause those symptoms. See if the development of tasks that give satisfaction won't reduce these symptoms.

Just because a child's immediate concerns might not be identical with yours, don't overlook them. This is a natural opportunity for you to build a *better relationship* with the child. Don't say to him that he has to do what other children do and that until he does, you aren't going to help him. Don't say that you think these things have no place in school. Don't say that you wish he would have fewer ideas and would pay more attention to what you want done.

Don't make assignments that may be ambiguous to some children. Don't give general commands that some children cannot carry out.

Don't create a situation in which you are trying to be the inspector of what *they don't know.* Create the impression that we are all there to learn together and that whenever we are blocked, somebody will surely help us over it. Give a feeling of confidence rather than of insecurity.

Some teachers notice that a child is aware of something that he has done that is not quite right and then they bawl him out for it. The child feels that this bawling out is an injustice. He knows that he was already aware of what he had done that was wrong. He senses that the teacher had insight into his own awareness. He feels that he has been punished enough by the awareness of his error and he resents the added punishment. We teachers can be sensitive to the situation and can avoid doubling or tripling the penalties for failure, thus intensifying the need for achievement. We are trying to meet that need and should avoid doing anything that puts obstacles in our path.

Don't get into a situation where children are doing a large number of little things and don't see the relationships among them. Don't have them work "just for you." Try to have them develop some purpose; otherwise they will not understand failure. Your rewards and your punishments will have more or less personal acceptance and rejection. You want rewards to come out of the child's experience rather than from you as a person.

Don't make the mistake of thinking that the only important accomplishment in life is excellence in reading or spelling. Don't lack confidence in yourself to explore some of the new media. Try out new things with your children and get some help from parents, other teachers and your supervisors. Don't give a child the impression that *unless* he can read well, his other skills *count for nothing.* These other skills are important too *and* so is reading, but reading isn't everything.

Here again we can avoid pushing children into activities for which they are not ready. We can avoid making the assumption that we know when they are ready and they don't. We can avoid making decisions which children themselves should help to make. We can avoid wanting a standard kind of behavior from all of them.

Here again we can avoid making too many judgments about their progress and excluding them from having some say in it. We can avoid telling them just what they have achieved and what they have not achieved. We can avoid being put in the role of knowing what their feelings are, but instead create a situation in which we can find out what their feelings are.

We are not to try to praise everything and anything out of relationship to the child's own standards, for he will soon find out if we are not intelligent about our rewards, our praise, our encouragement.

We can't fool him very long, and he won't have much respect for us if we don't have much respect for our own standards or for his. If children have helped to set the standards, if they have been asked to summarize what they have done and what they think they have achieved, they have already placed themselves in a position for rewards and praise.

Summary

We want to build up in each child a sense of inner security, part of which is built on the foundation of a sense of achievement, independence, and personal importance. We have listed a large number of things that can be done which are probable helps in building up this feeling of accomplishment, self-esteem, and being a person in one's own right. It should be said again, however, that any single one of these things, or any combination of them *by themselves* may not produce the desired effect. These things have to be done in a relationship where the teacher is genuinely concerned about the inner security of children. As she does these particular things to build a sense of achievement, she must do them in a way that reflects real concern for a particular child's inner security. It is only as she is working on the central idea that her activities have meaning, and a child can sense whether these are mechanical activities, or warm and *genuine* ones that are concerned with his own growth and development as a person. Here again, a sense of trust and confidence in each other is vital.

III. MEETING THE NEED FOR ECONOMIC SECURITY

In order to understand the child's need for economic security we must remember that in the very earliest days of his life the growing infant experiences many "economic" relationships with his mother. When the food is good and *when there is a regularity about getting it,* when there is a *confidence that hunger will not go unappeased,* the environment is affording economic security in the sense in which we mean it. As a child comes to recognize the shelter in which he lives, he experiences that shelter in an envelope of warm friendliness in his life with his mother, and he comes to expect that that particular shelter will be *sure and continuing.* Economic security seems to be *continuity* of that which has sustained life in a warm and trusting relationship. As the child grows in this kind of atmosphere he senses a continuity about other necessities: clothing, toys, adornments, and added pleasures. This continuing stability of the given environment is associated with pleasant relationships, and a sense of economic security builds a confidence that these requirements will be met in the future.

I say all this because I do not want teachers to follow another interpretation that seems quite easily made. For some reason or another, some teachers seem to think that economic security is roughly equivalent to "social climbing," that economic security is in some way identified with abundance, or with having as much as the middle classes have. Economic security is then relative and becomes a matter of "keeping up with the Joneses" or else economic security is not achieved.

I prefer to associate the concept with *confidence in security-giving relationships* in which other emotional needs are interacting. We think of economic insecurity as an anxiety about the economic future, whether it is the immediate future or the long-time future. Where children are worried about their father's job, or are anxious because teachers or parents have suggested fears about the future, we say that economic security in the life of the child is threatened. Where children feel that these necessities of life are below the minimum for maintaining life and health, we say that economic security is endangered. Where children feel that schools and other social institutions are making demands upon the family budget which cannot be met, they indicate the feeling that their economic security is threatened. Where every purchase contemplated by a child is related to a budget that is talked about as if it were *in doubt,* then, too, the feeling of economic security is in danger.

There are many ways in which this feeling may be endangered. Sometimes parents are unemployed temporarily or have their wages or salaries cut. Sometimes there are extraordinary expenditures in a crisis, widespread unemployment, and rumors about depressions. In many ways children feel these dangers in the social struggle, and *if they feel insecurity* on the economic front, their inner security is threatened. What are some things that we can do to help bring to children a feeling of economic security?

Some Things to Do

We should be especially concerned about classrooms in which children of widely varying family incomes are represented. If we are not careful, financial demands that are easy for an upper income group to satisfy are unusually difficult for the lower income groups to meet. We must, therefore, take stock of any fees that the school is accustomed to charge. We must somehow or another see to it that textbooks, notebooks, pencils, crayons, and other supplies come out of a common fund and, if they do not, we must see to it that financial burdens are at a minimum.

We must be very careful about publicizing the contributions of each individual child to any fund-raising campaign. We must be equally careful not to make public the results of attempts to secure subscriptions, to provide seed packages, to make equal deposits in the bank, or any other project that becomes a burden on some families. We must be careful in the way in which membership is solicited for organizations. Sometimes we can organize all of the extra-curricular activities that involve tickets into one big organization. We can try to sell a single ticket that will be given for all public events. Children can buy these very inexpensively and on any occasion may sell their ticket for a particular event and thus perhaps get to see many things without any financial investment. We don't want to deepen economic *insecurity*.

In cooperation with other social service agencies, the children of some families now find it possible to get a variety of services that would otherwise be denied to them. If teachers make intelligent inquiries about these services, they are often in a position to help many children with respect to medical, optical, dental, and other professional services. This is also true with respect to lunches and sometimes clothing.

Some children are overwhelmed with economic disaster that has stricken their families, and they seem to have a sense of hopelessness about the immediate future. Talks with such a child, the study of great men who have come through such crises, sharing experiences with these children help sometimes to bring assurance. Teachers can help children to see that whatever happens to a whole country happens to all of us and that all of us working together will certainly solve these problems and that we need not fear them.

We can help children to see more clearly the part that material things play in what we would call the good life. So long as we are unconscious of the role of economic security, we are apt to go along with the idea that the amassing of material things is equal to success. If we do this, children then equate a feeling of economic security with the piling up of material possessions. As we work with groups and with individuals, we can clarify these values and help to show the different emphasis that people now place on the pecuniary rewards of a society.

Sometimes children are told by their parents that some particular object they want to buy cannot now be purchased, that it must be postponed because of uncertainty about the future. If the situation is permissive and children can talk with the teacher about these things, she can often reassure them in such a way as to ease deep feelings of economic insecurity.

In our curriculum we can emphasize the contributions that *all* categories of people have made to our success as a nation. We can help students to see the progress that groups have made as they have worked toward important goals. We can have studies of different racial, religious, national, and status groups. Our curriculum will make clear that in many, many cases specific periods of deprivation served as a challenge and not as a threat to inner security. Here we shall be helping children to see the role that material things play in the life of a group and in the life of an individual.

Sometimes we can help a child in a very private and personal way. We can see that he gets the money to make a contribution if it seems terribly important. We can sometimes see that certain children get tickets to a show, or to a concert, or to athletic events. We can arrange for a clothing exchange in our schools that will be handled fairly by representative parents so that clothing as an item will be less of a burden on some family's budget. We will do all of this very privately and with a concern for the inner security of the children with whom we are working.

There are many children who really want an opportunity to earn some little extra money, and sometimes are schools are not very sensitive to this concern. We should try to find out the needs of small children, and we should even take some initiative in helping to plan with them how they might secure some additional income no matter how small it is. As teachers, we might have jobs that some children can do. We might have friends who could use the efforts of the children in our classrooms. As we arrange this, we should not do it as a "favor" but as a way of helping both parties to the transaction.

Sometimes in our efforts to help an individual child, we try to get information about the parents, asking questions about their employment. Children are sensitive to this kind of issue, and we must do this with great caution and always with the safeguards of privacy. This is equally true when we are making inquiries about the number of people living in their apartment or in their homes. Our country's culture makes children sensitive about crowding and about "boarders," and we must safeguard their feelings of security.

In the past twenty years our nation's culture has taken a turn in the direction of safeguarding the social security of young and old alike. We may differ on whether these efforts are adequate, inadequate, or too extensive. Nevertheless, they represent a national policy that is directed toward reassurance. We can bring knowledge of this policy to our children in our classrooms and do it in such a way that it adds to their sense of economic security.

We can help children to see how education, special skills, persistent efforts, and sharing with each other all can help to improve an economic situation.

Sometimes as we talk with children we can give them feelings of security by convincing them that all effort is worthwhile regardless of the occupation on which it is expended. We can help children to see that the world needs all of us and can make use of all of us.

Some Things Not to Do

Let's not create a single unnecessary additional financial burden for all children in the room so far as common requirements are concerned. Let us not show our praise for those children who are ostentatious in their clothes or in their possessions. Let us not require school supplies that tax the finances of some families.

We should avoid putting names on the blackboard of those who did or did not contribute. We should avoid all references to the fact that "all but three children in our class joined" or contributed, etc. If we are going to put names on the blackboard, we should wait until it is possible to put *every* name there and under circumstances where participation has neither been forced nor had any possible bad effect on the families who are represented.

Where services of the kind just mentioned are available and are being distributed, we teachers must not embarrass children in any way that reflects upon the families who receive them. We should take every precaution to eliminate embarrassment.

We can avoid making wild generalizations about an unsure future. We can avoid saying, "Things certainly look black" or "You never can tell about the future; we might all be unemployed before long." We can avoid intensifying already existing fears by not adding new ones that deal with the economic situation.

Here again the "reading and writing" curriculum sometimes keeps us from identifying the concerns of children. We can avoid the fixed, rigid subject matter boundaries. We can get children to talk about their worries and, in the discussion, they find reassurances from others and the teachers.

We can avoid giving the children the idea "that the poor will always be with us," that the present situation will continue indefinitely, that there is no hope for change. We can keep alive the idea that through individual and group effort these things can be remedied.

Let us not make the common mistake of judging people by their wealth, their clothes, or their possessions. Let us not, by any slip of the tongue or unconscious process, communicate to children that the better people are always the richer people.

We must not communicate to children the idea that certain social classes, or certain races, or certain religions are "the best" and will likely remain so. We must avoid giving the impression that differences imply that one is always better than the other.

Some of us are unconcerned about the economic lives of our children. We must not be insensitive to their need for participation, and we must look at the structure of our school to see that it is organized in a way to distribute economic justice.

As we try to bring an increased income to some families or to some children, we must avoid publicity associated with it and we must avoid every bit of "talking down" to the individuals concerned.

We must not think of every extra-curricular activity that involves money in isolation from the total school year's expenditures. We must not add another, and another, and another on the assumption that each one is only a slight burden. It is the totality with which we must be concerned and the relationship of each event to that total.

Inquiries into family life should be made as they seem necessary and not on an awkward scale as if the survey itself were useful. We must not insist upon collecting data which we will not use. We must not ask publicly for information that might embarrass children. We must avoid every opportunity that intensifies economic insecurity.

We can avoid talking about some occupations as though they were so much less worthwhile than others. We can take pains to avoid referring to some occupations as being "low down." We have to be careful in our references to all occupations because we might be thwarting the feelings of economic security of some children whose parents are in those occupations. We must be careful to avoid any slurring remarks about people who are on relief or about those who receive assistance from our organized social services. We can avoid giving the impression that social services are something that no self-respecting family would share in. We can help children to see that self-respecting families ask for these services when they are indeed needed and that no loss of self-respect occurs because of the request.

It is not fair to represent our entire culture as one based upon more or less cutthroat competition. We cannot say that it is every man for himself. We must avoid making use of these phrases in situations where they do not apply and where they may have bad effects on children's feelings of economic adequacy.

Summary

In this section we have indicated again a variety of things that teachers can do which *might* help to bring up feelings of economic security. These things must be done, however, in an atmosphere in which the chief concern is the inner security, and not the material possessions. We are not trying to make social climbers out of children. We are not trying to encourage indolence or lack of effort. We should be trying to build emotional security. All of the things that have been suggested in this section should be carried out in such a way that the child comes to feel stronger and more secure in his inner life. Unless we do that, we have failed with respect to meeting this need for economic security. Our compassion, our love, our trust, must all be involved.

IV. MEETING THE NEED TO BE FREE FROM FEAR

We teachers must be careful not to identify "fearfulness" with the so-called "sissy type" of children. It isn't only the whining, crying, wheedling type of child who may have deep fears. Some of the more husky and more aggressive children are just as likely candidates. We are not sure whether some fears are inherited along with one's constitution or one's personality. We do know that in the earliest moments of life, loud noises seem to produce behavior that is characterized as fearful. We also know that a large part of the insecurity of childhood is related to real and imaginary fears. These fears seem to create tensions within the body, and to relieve these tensions children act in various ways which tend to become habits. One of the big objectives in trying to reduce fears is to create a situation in which children may talk about them. Getting these fears out into the open seems to have the effect of discounting them to some extent. Becoming aware that other children have fears seems to be a help. Becoming aware of the difference between caution and fear is another help. When children begin to learn how to handle "fearful" situations by cautious approaches, by preparation and readiness, they are also being helped to handle their fears and to make their inner life more secure. No child can develop positive personality traits if he lives under an intense pressure of fear. When he feels helpless to deal with his fears, he is inhibited in his efforts to learn and he shrinks from undertaking activities because of the tensions created. The real and imagined fears of children are often more intense than those of adults. Their vivid imaginations can conjure up horrors that are terrifying. What are some of the things we teachers can do to reduce fears?

Some Things to Do

Some children are fearful that they will not reach the standards that are set. This is particularly true when the teacher's unconscious or conscious behavior suggests penalties if they do not achieve certain standards. Children may have been humiliated in the past when their oral responses were commented upon negatively, and they developed a fear about reciting or speaking before others. We can be sure to relate ourselves to children in such a way that when they fall short of *our* expectations, that gap will not be accompanied by threats or admonitions which could leave a trace of fear.

Over and over again it will be wise for teachers to emphasize that some of the common dangers of everyday life are not to be deeply feared, but to be intelligently handled. Teachers can seize every opportunity to show that knives or scissors can be dangerous, but that handled well, they are not dangerous at all and are very useful tools. They can point out that traffic in the street can be dangerous for children only if one does not protect one's self and use caution. The idea is to help children see that fear can be reduced by careful consideration of the situation and planning for it. The teacher can greatly help "fearful children" by returning again and again to this theme with many different topics as illustrations.

In your school help to develop a policy whereby body-contact games are played by children of about the same weight or body types. Children who are small and light in weight may develop fears of large people by being thrust into games where they have to compete against heavier classmates. In general, try to make competition voluntary and to control it by having those who are approximately equal in ability and strength compete with each other.

Some teachers convey an impression of deep fear about germs. They emphasize dangers of contamination from dirty hands, from eating unwashed fruit, or drinking from a cup that another person has used. Some children take this so seriously that it inhibits them from eating pleasantly. They become afraid of germs. Teach them caution; don't scare them.

A child is not in a good position to learn when he is keeping his attention focused on what might happen if he doesn't learn. He should be free to pay attention to what he is doing. Avoid name calling, threatening children, and hitting them as means of effecting changes in behavior. Try to reduce your own aggression as much as you can: As you do, children are more likely to become more relaxed, less fearful, and more ready to learn.

Some children tend to do "dangerous" things. They run down the stairways; they sit on the window sills; they eat chalk and erasers and even paper at times. Your counseling in these situations should be soft and gentle and not tinged with horror.

There are times in school when some child cuts his finger, breaks his arm, bruises himself in some way or another, and a good mental attitude on the part of teachers can leave an impression of wholesome ways of meeting these situations. Instead of spending our time acting scared, being scared, or scaring children, we need to help in analyzing the situation, doing what should be done, and perhaps drawing a lesson from it.

During the school hours there are times when storms occur. Thunder rumbles and the lightning flashes. The way in which a teacher responds to these natural phenomena is communicated to children. Sometimes teachers explain some of their own fears to children and try to explain how these fears originated in their own childhood, and they tell the children how silly they are and how irrational they may be. They explain their present actions as habits contracted in early childhood. They try to point out that this new generation of children growing up will probably not have these fears, or, at least, not have such intense ones. Try to anticipate the coming of storms and try to anticipate your reactions to it.

Sometimes fears are reduced as children try to make an objective study of them. Every year the curriculum might include some unit on common fears. As children begin to study storms, as they study germs, as they study traffic, they come to know something about causes and effects. This understanding of what is taking place can act as a reducer of fear.

Children's fears are real and important to them. As they give you some evidence of fear, respect it. Help them to get it out. Be dignified about it and pay attention to what they are saying; be sympathetic to the first expression of those fears. Children won't express them unless there is a strong pressure from their own inside, and when they do express them, take them seriously.

Sometimes teachers can suggest to children that if they have some fears they want to talk about, they should come to them privately and raise the whole question. They communicate to children the idea that talking over fears is often a help and that any time the children have such things to discuss, they will be glad to meet with them.

In these troubled decades, many children are growing up in an atmosphere of war. Teachers have a heavy responsibility to develop the best mental hygiene possible in these difficult situations. Facts about war, about death rates in wars are sometimes helpful. Reassuring children that strong movements are at work to secure peace is sometimes helpful. Reassuring children that in dangerous times we are all brought closer together sometimes makes for added security. These fears of wars, fears of atomic bombs and unknown fears of the future are serious phenomena. Calm, deliberating discussions can sometimes be helpful.

There is evidence from the great religions of the world of the tremendous force of love and good will in the world. There is literature which abounds with great names and the work of groups which are dedicated to friendliness to all mankind. Children should come to know about the many individuals and organizations who are working for good will and friendliness among all peoples.

Some children are afraid of *new* ideas because they are new. Some children are afraid of new toys, new assignments, new acquaintances. These children have learned to be afraid of newness and strangeness. Teachers can break down this fear by frequent mention of the irrelevance of the factor of newness. Teachers can help children to analyze the situation rather than to concentrate on the factor of strangeness or newness.

Some children are "afraid to be different." There is a tendency to want to be just like everybody else. This probably originates in our home culture, but many schools reinforce it because of a single standard of achievement for all children. Teachers may reduce this fear by pointing out differences that they like: differences between themselves and other faculty members and how this makes for a good school; differences in the books that are studied and how these differences make for a better reading program; differences in the abilities of children that make the room a better place to live and a happier group to work with. Teachers try to help children see when differences are good, when they are unimportant, and when they take on a negative significance. In this way they demonstrate to children that one should not be fearful of being different because that can make mediocrities of us all. In other words, they help them to see that the object is not to be all alike in every unimportant detail, nor to be all alike where differences make for happier living.

Sometimes children have deep fears of heaven or hell, of one or both parents or grandparents, of the dreams or impulses they have, of the opposite sex, of the future. Where teachers feel that the children's fears are so deep or so crucial about things that they are unable to cope with, they have the responsibility to report to school officials and set in motion that series of steps which might bring a specialist to the child: a clinical psychologist, psychiatrist, psychoanalyst, or religious counselor. These agencies also operate to reduce fears and we should make use of their services.

The whole atmosphere of a room and the schedule of work is related to the increases or the decreases of fears. There is time to relax if the resistance is not too heavy, if there is flexibility in the requirements, if children help to set the standards and help to enforce them, if there is soft music some time during the day, if there are parties and good times, if there is a general atmosphere of permissiveness and participation. This "totality" of things operates as an effective aid in reducing fears.

Working with parents, teachers can help to emphasize the important role that fear plays in distorting behavior. Teachers can help parents to understand the place of report cards in the lives of children. Teachers can help children to understand the relationship of achievement to their own growth. They can help parents to integrate their human relations with the efforts the teachers are trying to make. In their contacts with librarians, policemen, firemen, and Sunday schools, teachers can help to make their influence felt in this reduction of fear in the lives of children.

Many situations are charged with fear because we haven't the knowledge and the insight to understand them well. For almost every such situation, however, there are authorities who have written about the problem and can answer children's questions at almost every age level. Schools may invite authorities to come to speak to children, or sometimes there are very instructive movies that are charged with reassurance and understanding. The important thing is to sensitize children to the work of authorities. It is important to get children to loosen up their faith in those sources that are not good authorities.

The movies, the radio, television, and the comics all contain materials that can produce fears and anxieties. It is not possible for teachers to prepare children for all these situations. Nevertheless, it is possible for teachers to talk about these media for communication. Teachers can encourage children to talk about what they have heard or what they have seen and any fears that they might have derived from these media. As these fears become known and talked about, teachers are in a better position to help children anticipate the situations; they can help them to see "the imaginary character" of these situations and oftentimes the stupidity of them. Where teachers do this rather persistently, they are in a better position to share with parents the inferences they have drawn and the generalizations they have developed for the better guidance of children.

Some Things Not to Do

The goal itself is a reward, but not reaching it may sometimes be too great a penalty, and when it is then accompanied by threats or warnings, this increases fear. New ventures, new books, new assignments can be talked over with children so that they are ready for them. Don't make the mistake of assuming that fearful children need challenges. It is quite the reverse.

Don't scare children with respect to the everyday events of life. Don't tell them gory details of accidents. Don't tell them stories of how particular children have hurt themselves seriously by handling certain materials or tools. Don't try to have them do things or avoid things just because of fear. Help them to see that the use of their intelligence in a situation is their best aid.

Don't force children into competition; it sometimes scares them. Don't just "choose up sides" without having the children develop a basis for choosing which will make the sides relatively equal. When games get too rough, be sure that you exert some control and the children have a feeling that they will be protected if the roughness continues.

Don't exhibit extreme reactions at the behaviors of fearful children. Don't be horrified by their actions or shocked. Don't tell them "what is likely to happen to them." Sometimes while putting an arm around them or holding their hand, you can explain the role that intelligence would play in handling these situations.

Don't get "all hot and bothered" about a little dirt or try to scare children about germs. When talk like this arises, minimize the germ scare and emphasize the positive side of it: the use of good sense and intelligent caution in the situation.

Don't use unusual situations or incidents to make children fearful. Don't give the impression that this could easily happen to all of them at any moment. Don't be horrified at the sight of blood or show fear in the presence of pain. Acknowledge the painfulness and accept the complaints of the injured.

Some teachers get "mad" at children. They shout at them, bawl them out, threaten them, send them to the principal's office or otherwise isolate them. They make fools out of children in front of their age-mates or sometimes send home notes that result in punishment there. These teachers are using fear as a motivation. They are trying to change children's behavior by fear, force, or intimidation.

Don't avoid a discussion of fearful ideas. When these come up for discussion, don't start with "old wives' tales" as an explanation, but rather let the children investigate these deep concerns of theirs. Don't say that these things have nothing to do with the curriculum or try to minimize their importance. The best way for you to show that you think they are important is to include them for study during some times of the year.

Don't "pooh-pooh" the fears of children, laugh at them, or ridicule them. For example, don't say, "Here's a surprise for the class—Dorothy is very afraid of mosquitos." Dorothy might be trying to say something else to you, and the laughter of the class might act as a deterrent to any further expression of fears. Children are very sensitive and you know it better than most people. They don't want to be laughed at ever, and this is especially true about their fears.

Avoid as much as possible tense, awkward silences. Avoid, if you can, expressions of your own that will strike horror or fear into the hearts of children. Avoid superstitious explanations of natural phenomena. Don't talk about these things as punishments for some of our classroom behavior.

One of the bad things about fears is that they tend to remain private and secret. Evidently we are ashamed of our fears. Therefore, it is important for the teacher not to add to this shame and secrecy. Don't try to suppress these fears; don't try to avoid them; don't attach unimportance to them. Emphasize that understanding them and talking about them helps to reduce them.

If you can, avoid discussing the horrors of prospective war and the atomic bomb without reassuring the children that others are at work to eliminate these scourges from our society. If these things are brought up for discussion, stay with it until you see evidence that some reassurance is being built up that leaves children more confident in facing the future.

When *teachers* meet *new* situations in the presence of children, they can do so with a healthy, enthusiastic exploration. It is not advisable to be excessively cautious in approaching new topics or to emphasize how careful you must be when any new thing comes up. The teacher should not give children the idea that newness is something to avoid, but rather might suggest that as we grow up, new things are to be explored, invited, worked with, and, when they are good, incorporated into our life.

Don't emphasize hate, envy, greed, ambition, competition, and other such factors as the only motivations that bring high reward. Don't leave the children with the impression that the best way to get ahead is to step on other people. This often leaves an impression of fearfulness. Children become afraid of others, and their inner security is further disturbed.

As you point out that the behavior of some child is different, don't leave the impression that it is less desirable. Don't overlook the need for examining this whole concept of "being different." Don't reward conformity or conventionality as such, but reward it when this agreement is on something worthwhile. In fact, reward differences as much as you can and include as wide a range of differences as are really worthwhile. Your daily and even hourly observance of this practice will tend to reduce the fears of children who are afraid of being different.

Don't overlook the contribution that you can make in talking with parents and with a representative of other social agencies and institutions. A new era is dawning with respect to child rearing. Succeeding generations, if they are to be less fearful, will need the best efforts of all those who are related to the growing lives of boys and girls. Don't avoid your responsibility in communicating these ideas and exchanging your ideas with other people, especially parents.

Don't avoid opportunities for talking about the out-of-school experiences of children, particularly radio, movies, comics, and television. These media are affecting the growth and development of children, and it is not wise to think of them as unimportant. Give them time and consideration in your planning and work with children, doing everything you can to make children more intelligent consumers of them.

Don't just accept any old authorities for patterns of behavior or explanations of fearful situations. Where you are unfamiliar with authoritative sources, perhaps a committee of the children could investigate and find out the best available source. Don't let tradition itself become the foundation of wisdom or authority. Help children see that all around us people are examining these situations and finding out some relationship of cause and effect. Avoid the use of "false authorities" and the use of absolutes in general. Help children to see that work is going on currently and that keeping abreast of the times will perhaps bring us an assurance we might not otherwise have.

Don't keep the pressure on children all day long, having them concentrating at all times on intensive work. Rather than repeatedly suggesting goals, penalties, or rewards; and communicating the idea of "hurry, hurry, or you won't get done;" make use of the role of rest, relaxation, and variety in the daily life of a child. The decorations on the walls, the extra tables in the room, the arrangement of chairs all may suggest rigidity and tenseness. But sensitive teachers have found ways to use the environment to make for more pleasant living.

Don't try to handle *deep* psychological problems of children, trying to function as a psychiatrist or an analyst. Try instead to locate qualified professional people or get in touch with agencies and see what can be done to bring a specialist in to help.

Summary

The emotion of fear is powerful in the lives of all of us and particularly so for children. As they explore the world around them, new situations develop and there are many opportunities for fear to enter into their lives. We are seeking to help children grow into confident young people, confident in approaching new things and in exploring the world around them. We hope that they will be sturdy and unafraid, but we will not achieve this by any automatic performance of one act or another. The many suggestions that have been made should be carried out in such a way as to bring confidence to children, to reassure them and convey the idea that many fears are irrational and should be replaced by intelligent caution. This can be done when teachers begin to recognize that fears are important, and that good growth and development come about when they are minimized. The sensitive, compassionate teacher makes clear her identification with students and her trust in them.

V. MEETING THE NEED FOR LOVE AND AFFECTION

The earliest days of our life seem to have such an abundance of love and affection in them that they start us out with a general idea that trust and confidence can indeed be built in human relationships and that they are wonderful things to achieve. Indeed, those who have built these relationships seem to be healthier personalities. There seems to be in all of us a deep need for love and affection: There is some evidence to suggest that in the earliest days of infancy many more children die among those who don't receive a mother's loving care than among those who do. Whether inherited or acquired, this longing for love and affection and for a deep and abiding trust in human relationships seems to be one of the most important needs of them all.

In the pattern of needs that is presented here, *the need to be loved* is closely related to *the need to belong.* I distinguish between the two of them in the lives of younger children, and associate the need for love and affection closely with family relationships. In the early years of life and beginning again at about age ten or a little older, there seems to be a need for having this love and affection from the opposite sex. Where it is not achieved, there seems to be a greater proportion of abnormalities in behavior. The need for belonging, on the other hand, is associated mostly with free relations with age-mates, with being accepted as an equal member of the group. There is less intense affection, less intense warmth in the belongingness concept as I present it.

At all age levels every one of us, in our everyday relationships, must solve this problem of creating a feeling of satisfaction as far as love and affection are concerned. We seem to need very close relationships with some few selected people and sometimes with only one person. There seems to be a human requirement for deep warmth and for deep love in one or more human relationships. Where there is an absence of love and affection, thus frustrating this need, there are the usual consequences of behavior that is sometimes aggressive, sometimes submissive, and in other ways abnormal. What can we as teachers do to meet this need for love and affection in children?

Some Things to Do

Accept the feelings of children. If they are angry, let them see that you, too, probably would be angry in the circumstances in which they find themselves. If they are hurt and exhibit pain, help them to understand that you consider their reaction normal. If they are downcast and in despair, it is sometimes wise to let them see that you, too, in that situation, would be disconsolate. In doing these things you are accepting the feelings of children. You are reassuring them that these feelings of theirs are important, that they are genuine, and that they are to be respected.

In everything we do with children, we should try to be as friendly and accepting as possible. If they want to talk about things that seem to us irrelevant, we should take an extra minute or two to let them talk. We should try to ask a relevant question or two and try to show our interest in them. We can say, if time presses, that we can talk about it at greater length some other time.

It is important to let children know that you like them. At different age levels, this must be done in different ways. What is considered appropriate at the very early age levels is undoubtedly inappropriate for some of the later ones. The tone of your voice, the sincerity of your questions and answers, the sympathy and gladness you express are all ways of communicating warmth and a friendly atmosphere.

One of the associations of love and affection is intimacy. This is a difficult relationship to establish. With the special children whom you are trying to help it is a process of slow growth. You should understand, however, that you are working toward a time when you can share some of your inner life with these children. You become "confidential" with them, and as they see this relationship developing they realize that something is being built that is associated with trust and confidence. You are helping to meet a need for love and affection.

Sometimes you become aware that a new baby is expected at home. These are critical times for children who need love and affection for they will probably think that they will lose much with the arrival of a new member in the family. Talk with parents about preparing the youngster for the new arrival. Find out ways of helping to prepare the child for situations like this. Help him to understand it as a mark of his own maturity, and help him to see how he can contribute to the family in these times.

Be sure to identify as best you can the children who are in great need of love and affection. With these children create special situations, perhaps private ones, in which you can lavish some love and affection upon them.

Sometimes children offer us little presents and if we are not careful, we may offend them by our refusals or by the way in which we accept these gifts. If they can see that we are made happier by the attention, they will feel warmer inside. This helps to cement the trusting relationship that we are after.

If it can be done in a pleasant fashion, some children are pleased if you become interested in their family. Sometimes you can meet with the parents and talk in such positive terms about the future possibility of growth and development that the parents communicate to the child your great concern. The reverse is also true. As you build up the parents in the eyes of the child, he may come to transfer some of that to himself. As he sees your respect for his parents, he comes to believe that there is some warmth in your relationship with him.

Some children who need love and affection stuff themselves with candy, extra desserts, and with extra calories generally. They are getting "sweetness" through sweet things to eat even if they can't get it in their human relationships. Be sensitive to these obese children.

They are particularly in need of friendliness and warmth, and as they receive more of it in their human relations, they may be inclined to seek it less through their diet.

After accepting the feelings, after acknowledging that you, too, would have such feelings, after reassuring them that these are feelings that every normal person would probably have, you might then explore the responses these children made to the situation and help them to see other ones. Help them to see ways in which they might have met a particular situation, but always let the possible course of action come from the children and then help them to choose the better ones of the possible alternatives suggested as things to try next time.

Some teachers dwell upon the sad side of life. They talk about illness, deaths, earthquakes, accidents, and they communicate throughout the weeks and months a general feeling of insecurity about life. The world is in a sorry state. This generation faces a worse situation than the preceding ones, and the universe is heading toward distorted and unhappy times. Classroom conversation is overwhelmingly negative. As teachers, we need to bring emphasis to the positive side. We need to recognize when the sun is shining, point out strengths in people, and not only be liberal in our praise and sensitive to the good things that children are doing all day long, but point it out more often than we do.

Children come from various circumstances; some are orphans and live with relatives; others live in foster homes, institutions, or homes where there have been divorces and remarriages. Some of these children are bewildered by the changes that have taken place in their "love relationships" at home, where they have been required to try to love a new mother or father. When these children want to talk about it, it would be wise for you to listen and try to build up the child's inner security as best you can. Sometimes the teacher has to act as a kind of parent in these unusual situations, and when the child, by touching your hand, or standing close to you, or calling you "mother" once in a while, shows his desire in this direction, it will be wise for you to respond in a similarly warm fashion. Perhaps you will need to do this only for a short time until newer relationships are worked out at home.

Another step that might be taken to build security has to do with the birthdays of children. This has been mentioned before, but should be stressed again in a discussion of need for love and affection. A birthday card, a little demonstration in school, or a party can make some children feel that they are being thought of in tender and warm terms. If it is done in the right fashion, it can help in the building of security.

There are some children who find an outlet for love and affection as they acquire a new pet. This must be done cautiously if the teacher is to be part of the plan, and probably should be done through parents, or with the child preparing the parents for an event. A new puppy, kitten, or canary may be the event in a child's life which allows him to express pent-up feelings of love and affection. Sometimes those kinds of pets that can be kept in classrooms furnish such outlets. As children show the kind of unnatural loving care of animals, don't criticize it sharply and say that it should be reserved for human beings. Some children don't have human relationships which allow them to express those deep feelings.

For a great variety of reasons some children get relatively little affection at home. Their parents don't talk with them in intimate terms. No one kisses them good night, listens to their stories of what happens during the day, or seems to be concerned with their disappointments and their failures. No one even wants to listen to their successes. Therefore their out-of-school life does not include much love and affection, so in school we need to provide opportunities where we can somewhat satisfy this need. We can listen, ask about their experiences, say good night in a friendly way and add that we will see them tomorrow. Our written assignments can give children a chance to write about happy occasions and unhappy ones, too, and then we can talk them over with individual children who seem to need to.

Sometimes it is possible for us to take a child home with us for lunch or to a movie, a concert, a ball game, or a picnic. If we choose those children who seem to need it badly, here again we shall be taking a step toward increasing inner security.

Be concerned with the child's absences and particularly with periods of illness. Having him tell you about it, thus showing him your interest in his life and his health and his absence from school, is a step toward warm, friendly relations. Keeping in touch with him while he is away, being concerned about what he does when he is absent from school are other steps.

Some Things Not to Do

Don't say sharply to children that they should not feel the way they do, or that they will get over it in a few moments. Don't say that they are childish to feel a certain way about a situation, Don't say to these exceptional children that after all they got themselves into the situation and that it is their own fault. Don't be aloof from their feelings.

Try as best you can to agree that these feelings grew out of their experiences and as such are genuine and must be respected.

It is a delicate point, but while we accept the *feelings* of children, we must not automatically accept any kind of behavior that comes as a response to those feelings. We must be discriminating. We must avoid giving children the impression that because we accept their feelings we accept everything they do. We can help them to see that certain behavior is not what it should be and that other alternatives are possible. We must, however, avoid nagging and "looking down our noses" as we do this. We must act in an atmosphere of accepting the personality while we are examining particular behavior.

Don't think that you have no concern about the emotional life of your children. Don't be afraid to show warmth and affection in your relation to them. Don't be afraid to put a gentle hand on some children and say endearing things, but be sure that it is appropriate for the age of the child and for the situation.

Avoid thinking of yourself as somebody completely separated from children. Some teachers try "not to get too close" to children. If you are trying to help a child meet his need for love and affection, you will have to get rather close in order to be successful. This means that you should not be suspicious of these children, that you should not be neglectful toward them, that you should not be hyper-critical of them. It means, instead, that you will continue to be trustful of them even though a few experiences have suggested otherwise. These children will probably try you out and see if you will be trustful even "when they are bad." They want the trust and they want it for themselves as personalities, not for what they do. In fact, when they are mistrusted by teachers, they seem to find confirmation of their inner feeling that "nobody wants them" as people. It takes time and persistence to build the relationship that is needed.

In your relationships with parents, try to avoid criticisms in your early meetings, and with particular children you might even avoid criticisms altogether. Indicate as best you can to parents that you want a cooperative relationship with them, letting them know that you have enjoyed the opportunity to know their child. At some appropriate occasion you can motivate them by letting them know if greater warmth and friendliness seem to act as a stimulant to the child. Don't try to avoid the parental situation—it is extremely important in the life of the child, and anything that you can do to communicate warmth and friendliness will add to the possibilities of success.

Sometimes as teachers we are more or less indifferent to changes in bodily weight. We seem to think that nature itself is accountable. We avoid consideration of the overly fat or the overly thin child.

Where there is an unusual disproportion in weight, it seems wise to give it some consideration. Talks with parents might indicate that specialized help and psychological consultance would be valuable. Don't avoid these problems because often they become worse as time passes. They can become unusually intense and frustrating at adolescence, especially for girls. Looking into them at earlier ages can often bring great rewards in human relations.

Don't reject the attempts of children to do favors for you or to make little gifts to you. If it is something that should not be done, be sure to take it up privately and do it with great tact and consideration. You probably can do it in such a way as to leave them feeling that you have been deeply touched by the situation and it makes you feel awfully good to know that they think this much of you.

You can be careful that you don't reject a child or push him away from you by trying to discipline and control your own facial expressions and the loudness of your voice.

Here again we must avoid as much as we can negative statements that include the words *you* and *yourself.* We should avoid saying "I don't like *you"* when the *work* isn't up to standards. We should be as specific as possible about particular behaviors. It is *this sentence,* or *that word,* or *this particular event* that you and the child will talk about together, avoiding those sentences that seem to appraise his whole person or personality. You are trying to avoid rejecting him as a person and one way to do it is to avoid these personal pronouns.

A child who suffers from illness is already suffering enough and if associated with that comes a feeling that no one misses him, he feels even worse. Don't avoid opportunities to bring yourself into closer relationship with a child who has been ill. This can be a rich opportunity to begin a closer and a friendlier relationship.

In general, we should not be Nagging Nellies. We should not be pessimistic, but should work with this new generation in such a way that they will look upon the world as a happy place to explore. With the help of each other and people all over they can do great things, and we should help them to see this possibility. We can bring in examples of fine relationships with people and we can emphasize contributions.

Let us not divorce ourselves entirely from the total lives of children. Now and then we can make a little sacrifice in terms of our own life and can invite children to share some of our own out-of-school life with us. We must avoid thinking that our responsibilities end completely with the end of the school day. We must avoid thinking that we have no obligations whatsoever to the after-school life of children who need love and affection.

We teachers can avoid criticisms of behavior that is on the affectionate side, understanding that some children can't reveal such feelings in home situations. We can understand the role that domestic animals and pets can play for an unusual child, and we can show our appreciation of a particular pet without revealing that we know the function it is performing. We can sometimes introduce situations in the classroom just so these children will have a chance to be demonstrative, avoiding being critical or shocked by such behavior.

In situations where a new baby brother or sister is arriving soon, it is important that the older child receives reinforcement. Don't glorify the new baby too much, overlooking this child's need for love and affection and warmth in his relationships. Don't neglect the chance to show your concern for him in these times.

Avoid giving children the impression that their particular problems are of no concern to you. Avoid as much as you can the idea that you don't want to have anything to do with their home situations or that you are unconcerned with the problems that arise there. Don't withdraw from children who want to be loving and kind. Evidently they need someone to love and they are seeking you out. Try to be as accepting as you can. Should you also reject their advances, their feelings of inner security will be lessened.

Sad as it may seem, some children's birthdays are even neglected at home. Some children don't experience those situations of greater warmth and affection that come at birthday times. We can avoid being indifferent to the growth of children. We can avoid being preoccupied only with academic affairs. We can be concerned with their whole lives.

We must avoid being indifferent to the shortcomings of the environment. Don't neglect to find out something about the emotional life of a child outside of school. Without prying into the child's life we must create situations in which he will be able to talk if he wants to. Don't think for a moment that the social out-of-school life is not influencing a child's behavior during school time.

Summary

The need for love and affection in the life of every individual is of tremendous importance. When it is satisfied, there is a core of the person's life that is secure and trusting and full of confidence. No matter what the vicissitudes of life, he has more courage in meeting them. This feeling of finding people with whom to share love and affection seems to bring an inner security that strengthens us in many ways. It is not in the performance of a single act or a cluster of acts that this relationship is built, but it is something that extends over a long period of time. It comes from trusting children and building up such confidence that they in turn will trust you; from being consistent day after day in your relationships with them; from your tone of voice, the way you walk, and the way you meet their advances to you. It grows out of your respect for them and for their life outside the school, and develops from situations characterized by trust in human beings and warmth and friendliness in relationships to them. These suggestions have been organized into what seems to be a consistent pattern which, when acted upon in an appropriate spirit, will lead to increased feeling of love and affection and hence to an increased inward security.

VI. MEETING THE NEED TO BE RELATIVELY FREE FROM GUILT

When children start to explore the world in which they live, they often meet situations for which they are unprepared, and as they try new ways of acting they sometimes do things that are not consistent with "accepted" practice. Sometimes adults in the neighborhood use this occasion to shame, humiliate, or debase the children. Little boys sometimes show a great fondness for other little boys; growing children explore their own bodies, or they take property or money under the press of circumstances where they have not thought of the probable circumstances or of other alternatives. In these situations, adults sometimes feel that the behavior is abnormal, and are so provoked that they embarrass the children and make them feel deeply guilty and ashamed of themselves.

It has been said by some workers in the field that one basis for good human relations is self-respect. It is implied that we can't have much respect for other people until we first have great respect for ourselves. It is further implied that when we see people who are disrespectful of others, there is some reason for believing that these individuals may not have much self-respect.

Sometimes children have dreams that reflect the day's experiences, and when they talk about them, adults are shocked. They are not aware that certain feelings have been repressed and perhaps are coming out in the dream life of a child. The action of adults serves often to make children repress more and more of their feelings, developing a kind of guilty conscience. We sometimes see an expression of it in the cases of truant children. When children run away from home or school, they are often indeed only trying to run away from themselves. There is an underlying notion that perhaps if they ran away to some new place, they would be different people. They are not running away from home but from some inward anxieties. A child who is overwhelmed with guilt feels debased and small inside. Sometimes he feels as though he alone of all his age-mates is nasty, dishonest, immoral, or stupid. This feeling of small personal worth or a guilty conscience makes a child emotionally disturbed and his behavior often shows that he needs help.

The development or prevention of intense feelings of guilt in a child depends to a great extent on whether he is judged by adult standards that he does not understand or judged by his own standards. Adults often say to children, "You should have known better," in circumstances where the child really did not know better, deepening a feeling of guilt. It is important to know whether the child understands the situation and its alternatives and then that he be criticized, not on the basis of knowledge the adult has, but on the knowledge the child has.

Unwise teaching in childhood often lays the foundation for an intensely guilty conscience and a troubled mind. The conscience-stricken individual does not have poise, serenity, or self-confidence. Conscience is largely a product of learning and training, and the teacher can do much to give the child freedom from guilt. The process of growing up involves the process of making mistakes, but some children have such abnormally high standards for themselves, usually set by adults, that they develop a sense of guilt when they don't or can't live up to those standards which are too high. Some suggestions follow by which the teacher may help the child to overcome these deeper feelings of guilt.

Some Things to Do

One of the big things that we can do as teachers is to help children see that nobody is perfect, everybody has made mistakes, and the mistakes of children are often those that can be expected of anyone who is growing up in a complex world. We can help children to see that we can be a little sorry for making these mistakes, but it isn't necessary to develop feelings of guilt. Instead, we must understand the mistakes so that we won't make them again.

A child's experience in growing up includes learning a lot of rules and regulations. In our preoccupation with other things, we often do not take the time to help children to see what the requirements of situations are. When they do something that is inconsistent with the rules, we then shame them or bawl them out. Instead we need to make sure that rules and regulations are understood by children.

Help children to see that "conscience" is in part the result of previous experiences, that it represents some of the things we have learned in the past. Help them to see that a "bad conscience" is appropriate only if one knows of several choices and deliberately chooses a bad one. When we choose out of ignorance, we should recognize that ignorance is the fault, not moral values or bad purposes.

Work closely with children who seem to have a feeling of guilt. Help them to be ready for the next situation. As you observe them carefully and closely, be sure to check for signs of worth and good deeds. Praise them every chance you get for the good things that they do. Be sure not to praise them just for the end product, because this might arouse such a desire for that praise that they will again do devious things to get the praise. Be sure that your rewards go for *the process* of achieving.

Sometimes we can help children to see that the past is the past and that we are now living in the present. We do this by saying that every day offers opportunities and we should make use of them. We also do it by having them talk about "past mistakes," analyzing them with children, and helping them to see that their lack of experience was probably responsible for any faults that were committed: that it was not their intent to do bad and that the learning that they received from it is a positive good.

We need to learn something about the behavior of children who come from different social and economic levels. There is evidence that the child-rearing habits of these families are very different—the rewards and punishments are different and are given for different kinds of behavior. The language that is used, the habits of cleanliness practiced, the clothes that are worn are often significantly different. As teachers, we should know that children's attitudes grow from their experiences, and the attitudes that they present in our classroom grow from their particular backgrounds. We must learn how to deal with these attitudes in ways that strengthen the inner security of the children.

One of the very first things to do is to learn to ask questions of children, to find out how they happened to do what they did, to find out if they know why they did them, and to find out if they know alternatives to what they did. All too often we are prone to pre-judge children without having the evidence for judging.

Be very sensitive to children who are running away from things in general, whether it is from home, from school, or obligations of any kind. These children are showing symptoms that may be associated with guilt. Our job is to recognize the symptom and then to be sensitive to that child's need for more self-respect and feelings of personal worth.

Some children seem to be preoccupied with topics relating to sex —vulgar jokes or pictures, sexual gestures, or sexual play. These are often indications of inward conflict. It might be possible, in working with the parents, to bring some needed information to the children. It might be more desirable to see that school officials are informed along with parents and that perhaps some psychological services could be brought into play.

As has been said before, sometimes a child's need for achievement is so great that he will even lie, cheat, or steal in order to get certain rewards from the teacher, his parents, or his age-mates. Then under certain circumstances, he is made to feel very ashamed of himself and very embarrassed *because he had this need for achievement* and because he expressed it in these ways. As children grow up they try these ways of achieving goals that are of great concern to them at the moment. We need to understand some of the causes of their behaviors, and this is especially true of the ways in which children try to achieve standards without working for them.

In our classrooms a situation develops in which some theft has been committed, money has been missed, or some article of clothing is missing. We teachers have special responsibilities for situations like this and we must approach the situation with complete trust of every single child in the room. We must be careful not to give the impression that we are suspicious of one or two, but rather that somehow or another this will be worked out, and that if a mistake has been made it can be remedied. Our language particularly should not reflect deep shock, but rather a concern that the problem should be solved.

Children tend to show deep feelings of guilt in being "bad losers" in competitive games. Sometimes it is wise to treat this symptom. We can help such children prepare for every competitive event. We can help by anticipating the probable outcomes. Sometimes when losing seems to be sure, we can help them see that a moral victory may consist in keeping the score down and in attempting to keep the margins less than a certain estimate. Or more important perhaps, we can point out that winning isn't the important thing, but rather enjoying playing the game and doing your best. It seems that the problem with competitive games is that stress is always laid on winning rather than having a good time.

The child with a feeling of guilt often picks on himself; he protests that *he* is not very good, at least, not as good as the others, and tends to run himself down. When he communicates these feelings, teachers should listen to these explanations and file them in their mental filing cabinets. The child is telling you that he feels guilty. He wants to have experiences where he can feel good and worthy, like other people. He wants to be assured of this, and our job is to create situations where we can notice these things and tell him good things about himself.

Some children seem to have been protected against failure. They have had a steady tide of success experiences. Over-indulgent parents and teachers have insisted upon perfection; anything short of that is regarded as a disappointment and sometimes as a failure. In your year-round work with children, help them to see that different situations call for different standards, that perfection itself is not always the standard. Sometimes we need to know the correct answer to a problem in dollars and cents. Sometimes our clothing should be particularly appropriate to the event and it should not always be the same for all events. As children learn to size up different situations and the requirements of different situations, they learn to appraise their own behavior more realistically and learn that our thinking is not always in terms of perfection.

Some children have the idea that adults have never made a mistake, that our lawmakers and our professional people grew up through childhood without ever having done a single misdeed. How some children get these standards or ideas we do not know, but they do have them. It is wise to help children see that our successful adults also faced these problems of childhood, also made mistakes, and were probably helped to profit from them. Teachers need to help children see that the present generation of adults is not some exceptional group entirely different from children who, day after day, are making mistakes and who are kept in ignorance of the mistakes that adults are now making and made as children.

Some Things Not to Do

Don't assume that a child knows better. Don't assume that you know what he wants, that you know his feelings. As a mature adult, you are supposed to be calm, more objective, and more considerate. Don't judge him before the evidence is in.

We should avoid "harping" upon occurrences that are past, bringing up again and again some things that happened last week or last month. We should avoid assuming a kind of permanent badness of character from a single behavioral situation.

Don't assume the children know the rules and regulations or that because they have broken them they have done so purposefully or with indifference. Don't assume that these rules have been taught and then forgotten, or that they have been taught recently enough to be remembered.

Don't avoid chances to talk about "conscience" and what it means. Don't always say that *ignorance* deserves to be blamed and that ignorant children should be humiliated or embarrassed. In school particularly, the erasing of ignorance is an important goal. It is our job to find the areas of ignorance and to replace them with informed knowledge.

We should be very careful in trying to avoid situations where we will make children feel ashamed of themselves, where they will feel inadequate or "mean" inside.

We must avoid standards that are impossible for children to achieve. We must, over and over again, try to help children see alternatives, and we can't do this by restricting their choices all day long. It is only as they see the possibility of multiple choices that more intelligent action will come.

Don't show shock or horror at the language of children or at some of their habits of cleanliness. Don't be affronted by certain language patterns that are characteristic of the life of the child's family. Instead, use it as an opportunity to present further alternatives, always leaving final choices to the child.

Don't bawl a child out for running away, for being truant from school, for running away from a bawling out or a conference. Don't ridicule him as a person who is afraid to take his medicine or meet his obligations. This is something like bawling him out for having a high temperature. He needs courage and he will not get it from being scolded.

Avoid giving the idea that outstanding adults were little angels as children, that they never did anything bad as youngsters. Avoid communicating the notion that adults never make mistakes, or if they do, that they are only minor ones. Avoid giving the idea that adults don't have feelings of guilt about some of the situations in which they find themselves.

Don't become horrified over those symptoms of guilt that are related to sex, and don't try to suppress them with force and violence. It is much better to be casual about it, to be as objective as you can, and to try to find out why this behavior is occurring. It would probably be better if psychological services could be secured, but even when you try this, be sure you do it in a way that does not deepen the child's own feeling of guilt.

When children lie, steal, or cheat, we can make a great public ado about it, shaming, humiliating and debasing them. If we do, we increase feelings of guilt and we are probably not helping the child to understand his own behavior. Instead we are probably increasing the inward insecurities. We would be wiser to make all these things subjects for private investigation, private interview, and private counseling.

In all our relationships with children as groups, we can emphasize over and over again that it is no disgrace to lose. We can show children how many times Abraham Lincoln lost before he became president. We can help children see that the analysis of a failure is often the basis of a future success. We must avoid associating defeat with disgrace, shame, and personal abasement.

Don't just say to children that they shouldn't have the feelings they do, that they should feel better, that they should be like other children. Let them see that their feelings came out of certain situations and that as they have experiences in your classroom, they will probably have different feelings and that as time passes by their feelings will probably change.

Avoid that old bromide that "we should always do our very best." There are lots of times in our lives where we do not make the supreme exertion and where something less is appropriate. Avoid the idea that perfection is the single standard, the notion that we are to be judged in every situation by what would be expected of us in the most exacting situation.

As much as possible avoid giving these children tasks which they cannot do, bawling them out publicly, shaming them or nagging them for their little and persistent faults.

We should particularly avoid setting up a situation in which we say, "This whole class is going to remain here until someone confesses," or "Everyone will have a sheet of paper and if he knows the guilty one, he will write his name on this sheet of paper. No one will know who wrote it. We will collect them and mix them up and then I will know the guilty one." These are ways of increasing the guilt feelings of practically everyone in the room. Other ways must be found in investigating these problems; otherwise we shall not be building for feelings of a clear conscience.

Summary

Feelings of guilt and bad conscience trouble a child inwardly. If he has intense feeling of guilt, he feels less secure, he is less able to meet life situations, and he is less ready to listen and to learn. Thinking that he himself amounts to very little, he is even more sure of this self-estimate when teachers seem to have little respect for him. It is our job to try to raise this self-evaluation, to increase his self-esteem, to develop feelings of self-respect. In all the ways that have been suggested, a teacher can help in this cause. It isn't any specific suggestion or any series of them, however, that does the work. All the things that you do must be done in a way that is related to this basic problem of increasing self-respect. The things you do must be done in such a way that a child feels more clean, more wholesome, more self-respecting. The activity is important only in terms of the way that it is carried out. It is assumed that you can be helpful in reducing intense feelings of guilt, and it is assumed that you will think of many things in addition to those listed above to help you in this important cause.

VII. MEETING THE NEED FOR SELF-RESPECT

The little child begins to develop a feeling of independence, of being a personality in his own right, during the second year. He begins to see that he is different from others, that he can influence their actions, and that some of his own wishes and desires are respected. This feeling of personal worth that is built up in the early years of childhood is evidently of great importance in developing a healthy personality. Furthermore, in this whole process a child gets the idea that he will have the opportunity to express himself, particularly where he is a member of a group and a decision is to be made by the group that will affect him. Sometimes this group consists of only two people, his mother or his father and himself, his teacher and himself, an age-mate and himself. Sometimes there are more than two in the situation.

Where a child feels that his ideas are not to be given consideration, where people look upon him as unimportant and leave the impression that the child is too young or too small to be taken into consideration, his feelings of personal worth are weakened. As was said in the previous section, if we think well of ourselves we have created a basis in which it is easier to think well of others. Where we participate in situations day after day and people deny us the opportunity for self-expression, we come away thinking less of ourselves. Children resent being pushed around. They want to feel that they have rights which are respected. They object to having decisions made for them time and again; they want to share in the planning of their lives and in the process of making selections and decisions. What are some things that we can do to help meet this need for self-expression and for sharing in group decisions that affect individual members in the group?

Some Things to Do

As teachers, we can ask children to share in setting up the schedule and standards of achievement, choosing some curriculum experiences, and solving the problems that come up for solution in the course of a school day.

In our teaching we sometimes emphasize out of all proportion the place that information has in school life. Learning information is one thing. Total living also involves learning to think and plan together, identify values, relate ourselves to other human beings in a friendly way, appreciate differences, explore the world, and establish good habits of health. Giving children choices to learn these things is showing a respect for their personalities. They need this varied emphasis in order to live a full life.

Be sure to give children an opportunity to help evaluate their work. Sometimes you might allow them to save their papers, or their art work, or their records of experiences. You might then allow them to choose from their total collection a sample on which they wish to be appraised. They will have to choose in terms of quantity *and* quality. Give them a chance to write out or say what they think of this work in terms of many factors. Listen to the individual children carefully. Indicate your agreements and, if you disagree, tell why.

One of the ways to build self-respect and a feeling of personal worth is to create situations where children will have more responsibility. Perhaps a committee should be organized with definite responsibilities; perhaps student government should be instituted; perhaps the curriculum should be one of the projects in which groups of children work together.

We can trust children more. We can help them to do more planning and then give them more responsibility in carrying on with the plan. We can ask for summaries of progress now and then, but not with the idea of "checking up" on them. We will accept statements of what they do as honest expressions of their efforts. We will then plan the next steps with them.

In every group situation where a decision is to be reached, the teacher may at times comment to the effect that some children haven't yet spoken at all. She then asks them if they want to say anything before the group goes ahead to make a decision. This is a way of showing respect for people who are disinclined to speak up in group situations, and the whole group shares in increased self-respect.

Sometimes we limit the classroom environment so severely that children are denied the opportunity to make choices of which they are capable. If the classroom is deficient in non-verbal opinions, many children will be denied the expression of some of their deepest values. Where you can arrange for dramatic productions in which everybody will have a part, and where some parts probably will be played by three different people at three different presentations, you will be showing that you respect the need for everyone to express himself. If opportunities for choices in the field of music, in the plastic and graphic arts, in role-playing, in parlor games are a part of the curriculum, different children at different times will get an inner glow that they had a chance to express something that is important. Much more will be said about the freedom to express ideas, attitudes, and interests, and the freedom to dissent in the next chapter.

One of the best things we can do in building feelings of self-respect is to continually examine each situation *with children* to see if we can put *different choices* before them. They should have the freedom to list additional choices and then should have time to discuss them and the freedom to choose from among the choices they have listed. This opportunity to express your own ideas and then to make your own choices is fundamental in building up self-respect.

Some Things Not to Do

We can avoid making all of the decisions for children, setting ourselves up as little Caesars and little tin gods. We can take stock of ourselves and frankly inquire if our decisions should always govern the lives of children.

Avoid the heavy concentration on a memory type of learning and information, on what the book or teacher said. Encourage the making of judgments, the interpreting of evidence, the planning of a solution for a problem. Give opportunities for the enjoyment of music, poetry, and the other arts. Don't make the curriculum one which respects only the verbally fluent child. Build a curriculum with children that shows your respect for many abilities and for many trends.

Don't always check up on the children to see if they did their homework, their reading, if they were talking when they shouldn't, etc. As children see these suspicions of yours their own self-respect is lowered. Don't debase children. Our job is to build an inward self-respect.

Don't let days and weeks go by without giving children a chance to appraise their own work and listening to their appraisals. If you don't provide for this, children are getting the impression that the work they do is for the teacher, and not for their own growth and development. Moreover, if only teachers do the judging, children aren't having the opportunity to learn how to judge, and feeling deeply inside that they are not gaining in this ability, they are losing some self-respect.

Don't set up a school organization in which children are forbidden to do anything unless they are told to do it by a teacher. Here children get the idea that their own judgments count for nothing and that the judgments of the teacher are the only ones to be respected.

Avoid taking for granted that the opinions of a few forceful personalities in the room constitute the opinion of the whole group. Avoid situations where these verbally fluent ones make decisions for the others. Sensitize the whole group to the need for opportunity for everyone to express himself.

Avoid the excessive "reading and writing" curriculum. Avoid giving almost exclusive importance to reading activities and achievement. Emphasize the all-around world of life. Avoid the preoccupation with the standard and restricted activities.

Sometimes we teachers give children many "either-or" situations and think we have given them choices. We restrict their opportunity to choose, select, and make known the alternatives that they see in a situation. We are affronted if children want opportunities to differ from us. We can begin to see that *they have lives of their own to lead* and that they must have opportunities to express themselves.

Summary

In this section we were concerned with ways of preserving self-respect and feelings of personal worth and of creating situations in which children could find pleasure in expressing their values. We were concerned with providing opportunities for them to share in making decisions that would affect them. We wanted children to have a chance to suggest the values by which they would live, and urged teachers to respect these values in such a way that the values would become the standards of individuals and groups. I say again that no single one of these recommendations and no series of them will do the job apart from the spirit in which they occur. The underlying idea is to build in children a feeling that they are free to express values, differences, feelings, purposes, and anger. The basic idea is that children are different from each other and that they have different interests and concerns. They want the chance to express these differences and they want to be respected in the process. Where decisions are made, they want to be a part of that decision-making operation. Moreover, it all has to be done in a context where the children feel that they are important human beings and that their ideas and their values are being respected. A teacher who respects them will defend them, trust them, and have compassion for them.

VIII. MEETING THE NEED FOR SELF-UNDERSTANDING

Growing children seem to be indoctrinated with the idea that there are adequate answers to all of their questions. In their earlier years these children ask, and ask, and ask again. Every child seems to want to make his life meaningful, purposeful, manageable, and understandable. He wants to bring the world into some sort of order. *He wants to see himself in a purposeful relationship with the world in which he lives.* As he grows older, he is brought into contact with seemingly unrelated segments of his world. He goes to movies; he listens to the radio; he reads newspapers, books, and magazines; he watches television; he listens to his friends, his teachers, his family, and his relatives. He goes to church. He learns about illness, death, accidents, war, unemployment, and divorces. He picks up ideas about race, social status, government, liberty, beauty, and wisdom. As he grows older, he tries to make some sense out of it all. He raises hundreds of questions and he seeks, always, some way of coming to grips with the whole of it.

Strangely enough it is in school situations that this questioning upon the part of children seems to decline. There is some evidence that sixth grade teachers ask many more questions than the children do, while there is other evidence which shows that first grade children ask many more questions than sixth graders. The child evidently asks questions when a situation permits it. The child forges purpose when he thinks that he is free to talk about purposes. When he feels lost in the world, when he feels that he does not understand his place in the world, when his questions are shunted aside, and when he still wants to know, he often becomes disturbed. Above all, his questions are the important ones *to him.* To help him become a more integrated person, it is absolutely necessary that we help him understand some of his own problems and his own relationships to them. Self-concept is very important.

In other words, the curriculum of our schools must take into consideration those questions of importance to children. Every child seems to be asked, "What are you going to be when you grow up?" The child's immediate questions go begging while we ask questions about a distant and rather dim future. These many different contacts with life, unrelated paths of it, have left many children with a sense of confusion, conflict, or uncertainty. *Each child seeks direction for himself.* Our job is to help him on the path so that he may more intelligently fashion his own purposes as he comes to understand the world.

Some Things to Do

In the first place, and perhaps most important, we probably should try to provide a permissive atmosphere in the classroom. By permissive I mean that we should try to create a situation where children will feel free to ask questions and exchange ideas and where permissiveness will be controlled by purposes. As their own concerns and questions come tumbling out, as they express an ignorance about our social institutions, our own social problems, we see at once that this is a symptom of a need for understanding. We will never see this symptom if our school is not permissive. In other words, unless we are careful, we will repress the symptoms, cover them over, and then say that our children do not have any problems.

It is possible for us to pay great attention to purpose in a rather disguised way and yet in perhaps the most effective way. As children work on group or personal projects, we can raise the question with them of what they hope to accomplish and why they think that it is important. As this happens frequently and children's purposes become formulated and become the subject of examination and analysis, the children begin to see that you think their purposes are important in the world.

Sometimes a question occurs in a context which seems hardly appropriate. Under these circumstances, some teachers have worked out ways of using one part of a blackboard for writing down things that are to be taken up later. On other occasions, teachers say to children who are bringing up large problems, "Could you and I talk about that later after school or during a free period?" Sometimes teachers say quite frankly and *wholesomely* that they are unable to help on the question, and they suggest that it become a project in which some outside consultants will be asked for help.

In our classrooms we can make an effort to secure more sources of information, both about the past and the present. Working with school officials and librarians, we can perhaps get more current newspapers, more magazines representing different points of view for distribution. We can select different papers and magazines in order to get a wider coverage of topics.

Some of the questions which children have are directly related to very important local, national, and world problems. These are issues of a very complicated sort. Many children are confused and troubled by them. Teachers and groups of teachers would be wise to arrange assembly programs in which people with different points of view would make these issues more clear. These programs would be followed by discussion periods and question periods. Then, perhaps after lunch, the children could come back to an assembly and present the questions that arose in their discussion groups, and these could become the object of further clarification. When plans like this are a part of the school program, the children become convinced that understanding and purpose are important in their world. Teachers are respecting their need for understanding and their need for developing purpose, and if it is done in an appropriate atmosphere, children come to have increased feelings of inner security.

Sometimes children ask questions in a rather naive and unsophisticated form. Unless we are careful, we will give the impression of surprise that they are so naive and unsophisticated, that these are silly questions to raise in school, that they are tabu, or that the child must be a queer sort of person to raise a question like this. As teachers, we must orient ourselves to an endless variety of questions. We must create an environment that respects the need of children for understanding and for developing purposes.

In choosing motion pictures, recordings, readings, or direct experiences, we sometimes have a tendency to choose only those that contain a "pat" answer nicely rolled up in a package. As teachers, we need to learn more about projective methods and how to set up situations that stimulate children to think of further questions, other values, and other concerns. As they share these indeterminate situations with each other and talk about these curriculum experiences in which there was no "correct" answer suggested, they come to raise questions worthy of further inquiry. Usually they raise questions of purpose, value, and procedure. These situations where they have to choose between several "goods" or to choose between several "bads" are so much better for stimulating thinking and planning than the stereotype situations where the only choice is between something that is very good and something that is very bad. Life is not like that.

If children themselves do not raise certain large issues as they work on their own concerns, sensitive teachers should raise some of these issues with them. A few are listed as representative, but there are many, many more: What are the different sources of truth? What are the different meanings of liberty? What explains the different economic levels among the families in our country? Are wars becoming more or less characteristic of human relationships in the world? What are the chief functions of government? Is it important to relate means and ends? Is it wise to carry on experiments with human beings? These are only a few and should almost never be discussed in the abstract. Sensitive teachers would raise questions like this in the context of solving problems of concern to students. Raising such questions helps children to understand the world in which they live and helps them to establish a firmer basis for developing purposes of their own.

The faculty of a school could possibly arrange with local newspapers, radio, or television stations to run a series of forums in which issues are discussed weekly through the whole school year. Some of these would be student forums, some adult forums, and some of them would include outside experts as well as local ones. Summaries of these could become required reading, or some children who attended them might provide summaries in an oral fashion. This could also apply to forums that now operate on national radio networks. Teachers should do this only where they can see opportunity to integrate this kind of thinking with the work going on in school. The object is to build an increased understanding and to develop purposefulness.

In forums, in debates, in projects, in committee reports, in panel discussions which deal with life problems, we can help children see that our society has been made by our ancestors and that *we* are *now* making a *new* society by *what we do.* We can respect questions about how it was made and how we are making it. We can help them see that (1) they can understand it and (2) they can influence it. We can ask them how they want it changed and why they want it changed.

Some Things Not to Do

When children bring up these concerns about the world and their place in it, don't say to them, "I don't see what that has to do with arithmetic" or "I don't think that is something we should take up in school" or "That is something that you'll learn when you get a lot older" or "That is not so important at this moment." Under these circumstances we are denying the child an opportunity to express his concern about not understanding the world around him. We suppress the symptom. If we want to build for growth and development, we shall provide permissiveness instead of repression.

Don't feel that it is weakness in your professional preparation if you can't answer all questions children raise. Actually you probably are prepared to answer only the smallest fraction of them. Avoid trying "to give the answers." Try to get children to work on the project; try to get them to recognize authorities—to consult them, to interview them, or to bring them into the classroom. Avoid embarrassing children who raise these kinds of questions. In fact, praise them for raising them and indicate that work on the questions may help all to understand the world better.

Let us not accept the present library resources or reading sources as fixed. Perhaps through parent-teacher organizations we can find additional funds to secure more resources and a wider diversity of viewpoints in those resources.

We must avoid the emphasis on "busy work" for children. The real object is not to keep them busy, but rather to carry on such work as will contribute to their growth and development. What part of this growth is related to the clarifying of purposes and increased understanding of the environment? As children work together, don't avoid raising questions of purpose and value. Keep everlastingly at it. And the children's sense of inner security will be further established as they clarify their purpose and see more clearly what they are trying to do.

Just because some questions or issues are "big" is no reason why they should be excluded from consideration in schools. The resources of almost every community are helpful in clarifying these issues. Don't make the mistake of thinking that assembly programs are to be isolated from the total school program. They should be integrated where they seem appropriate and timely. Give children increased opportunities to exhaust themselves of the questions they have about these issues and have summaries made by groups of children as the tangible result of presentation and discussion. Avoid giving the impression that these topics are beyond their comprehension, that they are not pertinent to their present education. Instead, try as best you can to help these children see relationships between their present lives and these world problems.

Don't make remarks about the unsophisticated, or the silly, or the stupid character of some questions. Don't give the impression that they are irrelevant or unimportant. Develop ways of taking them into consideration, or of postponing them, or of giving the child the impression that a personal interview will help him locate people who could help him.

Avoid complete reliance upon a single text. Avoid thinking of the textbook as the complete source of truth. Avoid a curriculum that consists largely of one point of view that is to be learned and repeated back to us. Avoid stereotypes.

Don't just add extra activities to the curriculum even though they seem "modern or progressive." The objective is greater understanding and a developing purposefulness. Don't take on new and extra things unless you can see how they can contribute to the growth and development of children.

Don't avoid the so-called big issues. In teachers' meetings and in your talking with other professional people in your community and parents, try to find out what they think some of the important world issues are. Bring these into the classroom. Don't be afraid of your own limitations. You and the children together can recognize limitations and perhaps solicit help from other sources. Don't overlook crucial issues, economic issues, ethical issues; don't overlook opportunities to help children understand the world in which they live. Our job really is to increase this understanding and to develop purpose.

We should not give children the idea that our society is now fully made and that it was made by some kind of magic and that it is not to be changed. We should not reject ideas for proposed changes, but instead explore them eagerly. We should examine the challenges the children bring forth, bringing adults of the neighborhood into the picture as much as we can.

Summary

It was stated that children want to understand the world in which they live, that they want to develop purpose, that they want to be contributing members to a society, and that they want to do it intelligently. Many suggestions were made as to ways in which teachers and schools can function to contribute to these ends. Activities as such, however, may have both good and bad consequences. So much depends on how the teacher carries it forth. If she is interested in the children's questions about the world, if she is poised and stable enough herself to inquire into new problems, if she is concerned with the purposes of the children and the expression of those purposes, she will be able to use many of these suggestions intelligently. She will carry out many of these activities in order to contribute to an understanding of the world, and as these world issues are studied in relationship to individual problems and concerns, she will pay great attention to the emerging purposes of boys and girls and will help these children to clarify these purposes, to place value on them, and to be more discriminating in the purposes that will guide their lives. She will be helping children in the development of a healthy self-concept.

IN CONCLUSION

This whole section has been devoted to suggestions for ways of meeting the needs of children. It has also concentrated on many things that one should avoid in order not to intensify these needs. It was not assumed that these particular activities are specific cures for specific needs, but over and over again it has been stated that the ways in which teachers work with children, the ways in which children live with each other will so flavor these activities as to make them work well or poorly. The entire section has been devoted to an effort to help teachers see the things that can be done to bring an inner security to children, a sense of trust in human relations, a feeling of accomplishment, achievement, personal worth, belonging, freedom to express values and to make choices, increased understanding of the world, developing purposes, freedom from fear and guilt, and feelings of inward health and vitality and wholesomeness.

6

SOME
FURTHER COMMENTS
ON THE
NEEDS THEORY

A number of distinguished students of child behavior make little or no use of the needs concept which I consider so important. This avoidance or rejection of the needs concept may have many justifications. A most general one is based upon the idea that no two human beings are alike, that each one sees, for example, what *his* experience has taught him to see, and this differs from what another sees. This approach leads to a point of view that "categories" do more harm than good in the study of children. One should not *come* to the study of children with categories; instead one should get the facts and feelings and values of a particular child's life, and tailormake a category uniquely appropriate for the guidance of that child's life. This newly made category would, in nearly all cases, be inappropriate for the guidance of the life of another child.

I too believe that no two human beings are exactly alike, but if I were to study thousands of human beings, I believe that the research would lead to general ideas that would serve as guides for further study—general ideas which might enable me to make more accurate predictions of certain trends of behavior. These general ideas and trends represent categories derived from the experiences of those who studied children. The students of man also have very differing experiences as they are studying man, but this does not preclude the idea of a number of common experiences, nor does it exclude the idea of a commonly accepted inference from their differing experiences. The danger of categorizing is acknowledged, but categories will live or die on the basis of their utility and worth and upon their social and professional validity. They are something to guide us in our studies; they are not chains to bind us.

Those who say that the inferences drawn from child study are unique with each particular child seem to be suggesting also that every such inference is a creative synthesis new to this and all previous ages, that the differences between one child and another are not only differences, but significant differences—so significant, indeed, that a generalization drawn from a large sample should not give direction to the study of another sample. I disagree with this generalization.

Others pooh-pooh the needs concept on the grounds that it is an unnecessary postulate, not very useful, and not very profound either. I know a number of psychoanalysts who take this position, and a number of clinical psychologists, too, who say that the needs approach does not *solve* the problem of the aggressive, withdrawn, submissive, psychosomatic, or the regressive child. These critics hold that all that the theory can hope for is the reduction of anxiety and stress.

At this point I say that I am not *trying* to solve a deep psychological problem, if there is one. My job and my aims are directed toward helping children to learn. I do know that aggressive behavior gets in the way of learning, and so do all the other gross manifestations of frustration. I am not trying to get at the very deep roots of what is wrong with a most seriously disturbed child. I may have an aggressive child in my room, and I may treat him in terms of some diagnosis I have made of certain emotional needs. I find that the aggressive symptoms *in our classroom and in the school environment* tend to diminish in frequency and intensity of expression, and that the child is learning to control this behavior in these situations. I find also that he is paying more attention to his studies; he is learning more, and he is interfering less with the learning of others.

If I suspected a much deeper kind of psychological problem I would want to refer the child to specialists for further and more competent treatment. For those less disturbed, I believe that the reduction in anxiety and stress may be just what is needed for a child to get better control of his own behavior.

Some students of human behavior reject the concept of needs on the grounds that it is unnecessary. Other categories are preferred.

Lee, for example, is of the opinion that all of those ideas ordinarily subsumed under the category of *needs* should be regarded as values. The concept of values is assumed to be a more useful one for many purposes, and especially for an understanding of human behavior.

On my part I distinguish between needs-related behavior and values-related behavior. In the former I think of aggression, submissiveness, withdrawing, psychosomatic symptoms, and regression. With the concept of values I think of apathy, flightiness, over-conformity and overdissent, great swings of mood and attitude, role-playing and pretending, uncertainty and indecisiveness in decision making, and certain tendencies toward *under*achievement. I believe, in other words, that the concept of values is a most important one. (We have devoted an entire volume to it.[1]) But I do not believe that it is so all inclusive as to obviate the necessity for an emphasis upon emotional needs.

Not so very, very long ago a belief prevailed in the field of medicine that *all* illnesses were caused by germs. That has been given up, and there is a recognition of multiple causation. Not too long ago many teachers approached a learning problem with the preconception that the child was having emotional difficulties. The present volume puts a tremendous emphasis upon the frustration of emotional needs and the possible consequences of this frustration, but I do not imply that frustrated emotional needs are the causes of all the difficulties in child growth and development. I have indicated my convictions in this matter; I believe that physical health, emotional needs, independent thinking, values and status among one's peers *all* play important roles. I would not want to eliminate a single one of these large categories. I believe that each one of them has something to contribute to the insights and to the competencies of teachers.

What about the usefulness of the needs concept? Here I have much to say. In practically every section of our nation teachers have worked with the concept and have found it useful. We must remember that what may be useful to a teacher may not be useful to a clinical psychologist or to a psychoanalyst. These latter professionals tend to see a client infrequently and always in an office with no others present. The teacher has opportunities to interact with a child many times a day. The specialists in psychological problems are trying to help one person to solve a deeply significant problem. The teacher

---

[1] *Values and Teaching* (Columbus, Ohio: Charles E. Merrill Publishing Co., 1966). On pages 197-200, there is an extended discussion of the differences which I see between needs and values.

is trying to help a child to learn in the atmosphere of the school. The reduction of stress and anxiety *may* be sufficient for the aims of the teacher, and altogether inadequate for the aims of the specialists in psychology.

We close this chapter with a word of warning. The theory is relatively easy to describe, and it sounds good, and it seems to have worked out in terms of the results of many trials, but it is by no means an easy theory to apply. It takes a lot of time and attention. It takes intelligence and compassion. It implies a deep concern for children and their lives and their concerns. It requires patience and consistency and persistence.

It does work out with a very high proportion of the children, but with some individuals, it has failed. This can be heart-breaking after one has put in a great amount of effort. And yet, isn't that a characteristic of all professions? Doctors don't save everyone; neither do dentists, social workers, or lawyers. We'll have our failures too, and yet, if we keep studying these matters, perhaps we can continue year after year to reduce the number of our failures.

Where we have clearly stated theories to put to the test, we are coming ever closer to professional status. A profession rests upon theories which are testable. If the evidence throws doubt upon the theories, or if it is in opposition to the theories, then the theories should be thrown out. Where theories are supported widely by intelligent practitioners of the profession, then the colleges and universities should begin to revise their training programs in the light of theories that are supported by well-designed field trials.

7

OTHER FACTORS INFLUENCING FEELINGS OF SECURITY

All of us who teach should reflect now and again on how much of a threat a new learning situation (in the presence of a group) presents to a child. To overstate the case, perhaps, imagine yourself in a faculty meeting this afternoon. The speaker (say, teacher) is determined that all of us shall learn to walk on stilts, and he has a great many pairs of them on hand, and in every case the footblocks are about five feet from the floor. He walks on the stilts, demonstrates how it should be done, and says, several times, that it is a very easy thing to do. He then insists that the faculty line up, step on a table in order to be at the needed height, step on the stilts and walk around the room. He may actually believe that he has taught us to walk on these stilts!

In this faculty situation most of the teachers have indeed listened and observed, and many of them, inexperienced with stilts, may very likely feel some palpitation of the heart if they feel under pressure to try. You may not want to do it at all. In fact, you may refuse to do it in this public situation in the presence of your colleagues. You may feel threatened by the requirements. Besides distaste for the task, you might experience some mild threat to your own personality, and to your adjustment to the rest of the faculty. I believe that there is some similarity between this illustration and what children feel in the learning of something distinctively *new* in the presence of their age-mates.

Whatever is being taught at the moment, if it is indeed *new*, it has an element of risk from the perception of the children. The profession of teaching requires that we introduce children to new ideas. This means we must disturb, unsettle, and perhaps mildly threaten the security of those who are about to learn. How can we do this artfully? How can we, at the very same time, do things that are reassuring to the learners?

We know that over the long run and in the majority of cases, learning is more apt to take place when the learner has a deep and fundamental trust in the situation. Children need this feeling of trust, of security, to offset the threat of what is new. There is a small minority of teachers who seem to take a special delight in creating fear, anxiety, apprehension, worry, even some sense of panic in the minds and hearts of the students. Does this mean that *they* would learn *to teach better* if *they* were similarly treated when different and perhaps new methods of teaching are being demonstrated or shared? I very much doubt it. In their own cases, they would want to be treated with consideration.

From what has been said it follows that an important part of teaching consists of attempts to supply feelings of trust within each learning situation. We try to do this in many ways, a very large number of which have already been presented and discussed. We do it also by our exhibition of patience with the children. We assure children that if they don't "get it" right away, we will show them again, and if necessary, again and again. We indicate that if they have any trouble, we will be right there to help them. We urge them to take their time. We do not try to scare them or to threaten them with probable penalities. In our relaxed manner, we communicate a feeling that we care for them; that we will help them as often as needed; that we are supporting them in their efforts; that we have patience; and that we are there to guide them. That is, we are there *to teach.*

If we are trying to teach some skill, we should be aware that children differ in the time it takes to achieve some mastery of the skill. To hurry children, to urge them to be masters after too little time, is to create *in*security. To leave the teaching of one skill for still another, when the first one has not been learned, is a way of creating unpreparedness, sometimes shame and confusion, and quite certainly insecurity. What's the hurry all about? Is it a device to harass children? And are they in the room for that purpose? In situations of this kind it takes no longer to be reassuring than it does to be adversely critical. Why not bring security to the learning process?

In a similar connection, one sometimes hears a teacher say to a sixth grade child: "You should have learned that in the fourth grade." If it's that important, i.e., important enough to demean him or her in front of the class, why not see to it that the child has a chance to learn it *now?* If one of our faculty colleagues did not teach the child this needed fact or skill or concept, let us remedy the error in the shortest possible time. Let us make arrangements for the child to learn it now, and let us not shame the child. Let us bring more feelings of security to the learning situation.

Thus far we have been talking about situations where children are confronted with *new learning tasks,* presumably set by the teacher. We turn now to confrontations that may occur between children, between child and teacher, or between child and parent. So very often these confrontations are accompanied by some feelings of anger, hostility, or fear. And it may well be that these feelings are a consequence of frustration. Why should confrontation represent a threat? Is it a fact that difference is thought of as inequality, good or bad? Are we afraid of difference, and when it shows up are we uncomfortable and perhaps insecure?

How could we go about developing a pride in diversity, a preference for difference and not a mere tolerance of it? Perhaps we should put a much greater emphasis upon the ways in which we differ, one from another. We could help little children to see differences in height and perhaps in weight. We could have them draw outlines of fingers or hands and compare them. We could do the same with outlines of feet. We could put photographs of the children on a bulletin board and ask children to identify them, and follow up by asking how sure they are of their identification, and ask why they didn't choose someone else to be the figure in the photograph. We could have an ink pad and paper and encourage the children to compare a finger print with prints of other children in the room. We could ask them to talk into the microphone of a tape recorder and then, upon re-play, to try to identify different voices. We might snip a few hairs from each child's head (with permission, of course) and fasten them with tape upon a large sheet of paper, and see how many can be identified.

We could have a discussion about brothers and sisters and ask whether or not they look alike, act alike, or in what ways they differ. We might make a chart of pets, showing which children have a pet or pets at home, and what kind of pets they are. The chart could be very revealing of likenesses and differences. A chart could also be made of the toys we like to play with, the activities in which we like to engage. The list could go on, and on, and on.

We could help the children to learn how we differ in our blood groupings, and we might have authoritative data to support what we are saying. We might have something to say about organ transplants, and how in these instances, differences now play a crucial role.

We might talk about how often we have moved to a new home or town or city. We might talk about our travels—by train, by hiking, by water, by automobile, and by air. We could write the different ways on the board, and alongside each category we could write the number of students who have had those experiences.

We could talk about the magazines, newspapers, and books that we read or have read, or the TV programs we like, and here again we will find great differences. We could try to count all the relatives we have, and this would surely make for quite a range.

What is all of this for, and what is it all about? DIFFERENCES FROM OTHER PEOPLE AND WITH OTHER PEOPLE USUALLY HAVE THEIR ROOTS IN THE DIFFERENT EXPERIENCES WE HAVE HAD IN OUR LIVES.

We have been leading up to the idea of confronting differences. Our values, our attitudes, our purposes and aspirations, our interests, our feelings all grow out of the life we have led and the experiences we have had. If we have a great variety of differences in experiences, we should expect to find that we would differ with many persons in terms of what we believe or what we think, what we like and what we dislike. Can we help children to see this? Can we help them to see that our past experiences, perhaps very different from the person next to us, make us what we are. And if we differ, so what? Shouldn't we expect to differ? We have seen how much we differ in a great many ways. So why shouldn't we, perhaps, have different attitudes and different ideas?

There is another "security" point in all of this for teachers. What is the *right* attitude to have toward an issue or a question? Unless one wants to be a hypocrite, our attitudes should be consistent with our experiences. What we have learned in our lives should guide us in what we stand for. With different experiential backgrounds, there are very likely to be differences in points of view. There is no reason to fight about this difference or to have long bitter arguments about it. Let us help children to see clearly where the differences lie, and let us help them to learn to say: We differ on this point.

Help children in a more effective use of language when controversies arise. It is better to say, "I disagree with that idea," than to say "I disagree with *YOU*." This tends to be in the direction of depersonalizing the argument and helps both children to feel more secure, less threatened.

We can be more sensitive to the ways children state their beliefs. To say, "I believe IN some person," is to remove the issue from reasonable discourse. The evidence for that kind of statement is usually *inside* the person making the statement. To say, "I believe that . . . ," usually allows the statement to be inquired into; one can obtain evidence regarding the statement. It is less personal, and hence, less threatening.

In the face of a controversy help children to ask the question: Does this impinge on my life? If it doesn't make a very real difference, why argue or dispute about it?

Sometimes we are able "to cool" an impending argument by suggesting that we should postpone it for a time, and often this means the end of it. Sometimes we can suggest that the difference is one that should be debated by the entire class, and that perhaps many children would be on one side of the argument, and many on the other. Then it is just another instance to support the idea that where we have had different backgrounds of experience, we will have differing beliefs or attitudes.

Finally, give greater emphasis to the idea that where we are all alike the world can be very monotonous and boring. If we were all alike, we would not meet a new idea. Imagine that! How would we choose friends? What would we do when we were bored?

You are really raising the question of whether or not differences of many kinds should really be prized, not shunned. As children grow in this capacity to see that our many differences grow out of our experiences, it is here assumed that they will be more willing to accept the very fact of difference. And recognizing that, and seeing how much more interesting the world can be when we do have differences, perhaps children can be helped to prize and to respect the differences that do exist. It may be that difference, or newness, may come to be less threatening, and that learning something new will be accompanied by few or no palpitations.

Many changes have taken place in our society and some of them have been great indeed. The rate of change has increased greatly. We may be helping children to accommodate themselves to the idea of change as we introduce them to the ideas of accepting the fact of many differences among individuals. They may come to see the possible dangers of so many violent controversies which have been shown so often on the TV screen. This younger generation may take the side of peaceful discussion allowing recognition and acceptance of many minority points of view. If we can contribute to a widespread reduction in violence, we may be doing one very important thing in safeguarding a civilized way of life. And feelings of security will be greatly increased.

For children to feel secure, the teacher's behavior should be highly consistent. Students have to be able to predict it and depend on it. They must be relatively sure of it. You can't be widely permissive one moment and severely restrictive the next; nor can you be gentle, warm, and accepting one moment and just the opposite a few minutes later. If you are highly inconsistent, students will not know how to relate themselves to you; they will be insecure, and instead of relaxing as they work and study, they will be keeping one eye and ear open. No two of us teach exactly alike; our patterns of behavior differ. Each of us, however, has an obligation to be reasonably consistent within our pattern when we work with a group.

Children need to know the limits of acceptable behavior. The teacher must let them know that there are rules and that he will hold them to the rules. There are, of course, exceptions for most unusual circumstances, but these exceptions cannot be examples of favoritism for one or a few children. It is a good idea to work these rules out with the group in the earliest meeting days and to put them in a prominent place on the blackboard or bulletin board. Children feel more secure when they know for sure what is acceptable and what is not acceptable. And they feel more secure if there are not too many rules.

Students need to feel physically secure. They ought to feel that the teacher is their defender in all times of trouble, discomfort, or danger. If a child has an accident of some kind, he wants the teacher's help and sympathy. If a child is threatened by another child, who may be older and bigger, he wants the teacher to intercede. If a child is not feeling well, he wants the teacher to be concerned about him. A teacher who comes to the defense of an individual child or an entire group is helping to provide emotional security.

Every student feels more secure if he knows that the teacher will not diminish his status in the presence of his peers. This means that practically all punishments will be administered privately. No child should receive the scorn, ridicule, sarcasm, or name-calling of an angry or upset teacher in a group situation.

Students want a teacher who can save them from extremes of humiliation. Nearly all of us have learned a great deal through the mistakes we have made. Sometimes, however, a mistake made in the presence of our peers can be terribly humiliating. Sometimes a teacher can very quickly assert that he himself is partly to blame for the situation. Sometimes he can restate what a student has said in a manner that robs it of its adverse effect. Sometimes he can turn it into a joke on himself. Whatever he does, he tries to soften the significance of the mistake in order to help the student over a difficult situation.

Students feel more secure when the teacher is relaxed and pleasant. They like to be welcomed in the morning and they like to have someone say good night after the last class of the day. Some teachers make it a point to shake hands with each child at the close of the school day. Others make sure to wish them happy weekends when Friday comes to an end. Many teachers have a sense of humor and share a joke or a funny story with their class.

Students feel more secure when the teacher's explanations, directions, and comments are clear and to the point. If the teacher leaves them confused, the students feel insecure. Students have to feel free to ask questions, to say when they do not understand, and to expect a courteous response from the teacher.

Students feel more secure when they are with a teacher whom they consider to be fair. "Fair" is a word that children often use when they make comments about their teachers. It may be fair to have a rule that all children must take off their hats when they are in the classroom, but it would not be fair to require all children to wear hats of the same size. We may require all children to work, but it is unfair on many occasions to require that they do exactly identical work. Assignments, tests, and examinations should be fair; punishments and praise as well as grades and awards should be fair. A teacher who is fair adds to the emotional security of the learning situation.

Students feel much more secure when they believe that their teacher is loyal to them. This means that the teacher keeps his promises and takes such promises seriously. It means that he will not gossip about them to other teachers and that he will not tell other students what has been told to him in confidence. It means that he will believe what the children say until there is real evidence which is contradictory.

Students feel more secure when school becomes a place where they can "live," not a place where they must serve time. Many kinds of behavior should be permitted so long as they do not interfere with the purposes of learning. Students want the freedom to stretch their legs once in a while or to talk quietly with their peers—sometimes to "do nothing," to be free from pressure for a few minutes.

To feel emotionally secure in the learning situation students need to feel wanted and liked. That is, they need some warmth and affection if they are to learn. They need to feel that they really belong to the group, that they are missed by the group when they are absent. They feel like rejects when they are sent out into the hall, into the cloakroom, or to the principal's office. They need to have their feelings of fear and guilt diminished and their feelings of achievement and accomplishment strengthened. They need a teacher who will listen and respond, one who is patient with their endless questions, one who is helping them to understand themselves and the world in which they live.

If children feel free to differ with one another, to dissent with the teacher on occasion, to think and to express their views, they are more apt to feel relaxed and more secure.

The room itself can add to or subtract from the security feelings of children. Is it a warm, friendly-looking, inviting place? Or is it a cold, barren, barn-like space? The harmony of colors in the room, the pictures on the walls, the arrangements of chairs and tables and desks can add or detract greatly from a general feeling of security. Are the plants more dead than alive? Are they attractive for this particular room? What about the bulletin boards?

If you have animals in the room, are they well taken care of, and is there an appropriate space for them? Some children are very much attracted to them and their presence in the room can help to form a bond of identification which contributes to a feeling of security.

Is the room a comfortable place to live in terms of heat and light and fresh air? Should it be "aired out" more frequently? Is the room reasonably clean, not in the sense of "prissy" clean, immaculate, but in terms of a general impression of cleanliness?

What do you do about birthdays? Do you celebrate all October birthdays, for example, with a party on some school day in October? And what do you do about those children whose birthdays fall during the months of vacation? To have parties and to play games once in a while make for a "groupness," a sense of solidarity, that adds to one's feelings of security.

Children tend to feel most secure in their own homes and with their own families. Could we perhaps identify more closely with families and thus increase feelings of security? Does the classroom have one large bulletin board reserved for family affairs? Are there pictures of each child on that board? Are pictures of the child's family shown? Are there pictures of fathers and mothers at their places of work? Are there pictures of family pets or family trips and outings?

If a child is away from school for several days do you try to get in touch with the family, and do you show your concern? This may add greatly to the security feelings of children—to know that you really *care* about them.

Sometimes children are molested, or frightened at least, by larger children while they are on their way to or from school. Some children are even afraid to talk about it. It may be wise for you, the teacher, to talk about it some time, and to suggest that if this ever happens, they should tell you about it, and you will take care of it. This is still another way in which you are the protector and defender of every child, and as the situation is taken care of, the children do feel more secure.

Sometimes boys and girls get into an argument and the argument goes too far; it is heading for a real fight. They may not want to fight at all, but the situation has gone beyond their control. They want you to interfere, to stop it, and they feel better about it when you do save them from the consequences of bitter fighting. No one has retreated, backed up, or given in, and you have saved them that embarrassment. They feel more secure when they can count upon you to help them save face.

This part of the volume is now coming to a close. Some readers may believe that we have put an over-emphasis upon feelings of security. The times in which we live may have something to do with this emphasis. These are times of wars and turmoil, of confrontations which children see on the TV screens almost nightly, of riots and disorders, campus rebellions and sit-ins, protests and demonstrations, unrest, unemployment for many of our citizens, and times of inflation too. There is insecurity in the air we breathe, and children breathe that same air. They hear messages of insecurity as they listen at home to the talk of their parents.

There are factors other than the times we now live in. Did you know that in recent years there has been an increase in suicides among children? Did you know that many teachers have complained that "groups" of children are harder to work with? You have surely heard of the increased use of drugs among children and young adults. There has been a spate of publicity about the boldness, the impudence, the uncontrollability of children, their lack of respect for teachers, parents, policemen, and their elders, in general.

Did you know that one-fifth of the families of the United States move every year, and can you imagine the insecurity this might engender among the children on the move? Did you know that ulcers amongst children are on the increase? Did you know that more young people are "run-a-ways," truants from home and school?

Did you know that more than one-sixth of the families of the United States represent "broken" homes in one way or another: divorce, separation, death, desertion, or institutionalization? Did you know that women now represent between forty and fifty percent of the total work force of our country, and that for a great many children the mother is not at home when the children arrive from school? In many instances no one is there; in other instances there is a sitter, and in still others, a relative with little liking for the task.

Did you know that there has been an increase in the reports of cases which deal with child abuse by parents? Did you know that teen-agers and young adults commit the large majority of reported crimes?

Did you know that in a very much publicized report on the public schools of our country statements were made to the effect that life in our classrooms was grim and joyless? Did you know that one of our best known anthropologists, after studying child-rearing practices in several countries, came to the conclusion that here in the United States *we do not place a high value on our children?*

More items of a similar kind could be reported here. Do you believe that under these circumstances, we should indeed emphasize security for children, joy for children, power for children, freedom for children, and rich experiences for them? We can do no less, and we should get to work on the tasks before us.

8

COMPETITION
AND FEELINGS
OF SECURITY

Many ways have been mentioned that can contribute to increased feelings of security on the part of youngsters. The major part of the volume has been given over to the needs theory and to the dos and don'ts of the needs theory. There the emphasis was upon the emotional needs of children. At the conclusion of that section, twenty additional suggestions were made which were assumed to bear upon feelings of security.

In this section I discuss, perhaps too briefly, some of the factors related to the control and lack of control of competition in our society, and I bring the work of the schools into relationship with some industrial practices. I suggest that in many ways we may be lagging behind the culture as we stress competitive ways of working, and the competing for awards, grades, prizes, and praise.

The so-called competitiveness of American life is said to be a serious and adverse influence on the quality of human relationships in our society—the sense of feeling secure. As individuals try to excel each other, to win, to beat each other, they tend to elevate the goal as the most important value, and as they compete for those kinds of ends, they tend to under-value the worth of human beings. As the competition becomes ever more keen and the rivalry greater, this

132

discrepancy between means and ends is ever further heightened. Those who want to reduce competition in the affairs of man say that this reduction will be accompanied by an improvement in human relations, between individuals and also between groups, minority and otherwise.

Those who speak for competition seem to believe that the finest personalities are created by the process of competition. They hold that it is in the contest itself that character is formed and developed. It is implied that through competitive struggle for the same individualistic goal or prize, individuals are best able to "test" their ideas, abilities, and capacities. It is said that through competition, for material things as well as individual goals, the very best in our society comes to be noticed. Competition is assumed to be a process which helps to distinguish leaders from followers, the biologically best from those who should go down in the "struggle for the survival of the fittest."

Arguments for and against are not without heat and often not without light, too. Most frequently, however, the assumption is made that American economic and social life is a competitive *system* that characterizes and dominates *all* of the activities of our cultural institutions. Where it does not so characterize them, some speakers and writers suggest that a radical departure is being made from "The American Way of Life." Schools are urged to be skeptical of procedures which emphasize cooperativeness, sharing, or joining efforts on the part of students toward a common goal. Those who advise along these lines do so on the assumption that the values we cherish about our life in the United States (and the world) will be threatened if we do not, indeed, emphasize competition in our daily classroom living. As these people add up the advantages and disadvantages of competition, they find the scales very much in favor of "struggle with each other" as the foundation of progress.

In such situations as this, a very distinguished governor of New York State used to say: "Let's look at the record." Is our American way of life *a system* of competitive relationships? We have only to take the most superficial look to see that it is not altogether competitive in the sense in which the term is used here. There has been a remarkable growth in the number and size of cooperative organizations. Organized trade unions have increased in number, size, and influence. State and federal aid have increased and will probably increase even more. Cooperative efforts to extend opportunities for education to more people of all ages is a recent trend. Our government is, in theory, an example of cooperative effort in operation. The same may be said of our schools, our post offices, our highways, our departments of public health, and a host of other social institutions. In other words, we in the schools must clearly see that the United States does not operate under an inflexible, absolutely binding system of competition. More than anything else, our culture seems to be guided by *a faith* rather than a system. We have a society that has much competition within it, but a society which makes room for change. We have a society that provides for innovations while it is functioning. Recognizing that individuals and groups differ, we have a culture that allows difference to express itself. We might wish that there were *more* opportunity for differences to function, but it cannot be reasonably denied that our economy allows for many types of cooperative effort.

In this respect, schools reflect the social order. The central values of a culture tend to be operative in the schools of that culture. *Sometimes, however, the schools themselves lag behind a dynamic society.* Are there some respects in which our own schools may not be representative of the best thinking about competition as this term has been conceived and operated upon by other institutions of our society, including industry? What are some of the criteria which should govern competitive efforts? What are some of the answers to this question which are reflected in the present operations of much of American business and industry?

1. *Should competition be voluntary on the part of those who compete?*

Those who elect to start an industrial enterprise are under no compulsion to do so. Those who elect a certain occupation are under no compulsion to make that particular choice as a field in which to compete. Men are free to choose the area in which they will compete against their fellows, and whether or not they wish to engage in competitive efforts. Is this same choice available to all children in our schools so far as activities in which they may choose to engage? Are they free to choose where and when and under what circumstances they will enter into competition? If not, the schools in which they are enrolled are to that extent departing from prized industrial practice in our culture. Are they, then, increasing feelings of insecurity?

2. *After deciding to compete, are children free to limit the areas in which they will continue to participate?*

Industrial enterprise does not dictate to the entrepreneur that he must compete against *all comers* in *every* event. The retailer may choose where he will put the emphasis on his competitive efforts.

The largest industries tend to follow the principle of a distribution of intensity of effort so far as competition is concerned. Can we say the same for our schools? Do we tend to set up a situation *throughout the entire school day* where we expect *every pupil* to be a competitor for grades, marks, rewards? Or do we provide choices of times and subjects when, and conditions under which, every individual may elect to be a competitor? If not, we may indeed be lagging behind the American culture which has already—in a number of institutions, including industry—made such provisions for choice on the part of people who are associated with them. What is the situation within the schools? Are we creating feelings of trust and security?

3. *Is the competitive situation apt to be devastating in its effects on the people who are participating?*

If the outcomes of a competitive situation are apt to have a terrible effect on the personalities of those who are in the contest, then caution is certainly to be urged. American commerce and industry are now characterized by the caution with which it husbands its resources for continuing service. If management should stake all of the company's resources on a single throw of the dice, that management would be promptly replaced. In the past there have been many leaders (many in number—not in proportion) who worked in terms of hoping to hit the jackpot! But the trend in industry is toward caution with respect to gambling everything on the outcomes of any single project. Care is taken that the consequences of competition will not threaten the whole enterprise. Plans are most carefully drawn for whatever competitive efforts are to be expended. Preparation is made in terms of trying to be ready, and in terms of being able to meet the consequences of the action. What can we say about this in terms of our public schools? Do we protect persons as well as industry does in the competitive fields in which we operate? Do we plan carefully to anticipate consequences of competition and make ourselves ready to avoid some and endure others? Are we lagging behind the culture in this respect? What is the situation within the schools? Do we value feelings of trust and security for our children?

4. *Are the goals of competition flexible and changeable?*

Industrial enterprise in America is characterized by the freedom to set one's goals for one's self. A certain industry may not be trying to out-sell every other industry in the field. It may not be trying to produce the very best merchandise in the field. It may be trying to gain so many more units of sales compared to the record of last year.

It may have different standards with respect to different competitors. By analogy and within our schools, our basketball team may not be setting for its goal the winning of every game. There may be some teams scheduled who are so much better than we that it would be almost foolish to have our team set its heart on victory. Under these circumstances do we help our team to set up more realistic goals? Do we help them to see that they might, in this competitive situation, try to hold the defeat down to a margin of ten or twenty points, and hence compete for something that has practical and realizable meaning for them? Do we do this same kind of thing in our academic classrooms, this making of reasonable goals and providing for change as situations change? Our culture is pointing the way; business has taken that path. Are the schools lagging behind? Are they making children more tense, more competitive, more insecure?

5. *Are the conditions of the competition under reasonable control?*

This is a most important point and leaders in business and industry have done much to make competition less hazardous for many of us who are at times on the sidelines. If the competition leads to practices which threaten the safety or the health, lives, and feelings of other people, it is competition that is losing favor with American cultural practices. Muckrakers, legislators, educators, teachers, writers, labor leaders, and many others have been sensitive to the conditions under which goods and services have been competitively produced, and they have pointed in horror to some of the attendant circumstances and some of the consequences to group life as a whole. Out of these revelations has come an increased sensitivity to the conditions under which people will function in the area of competitive effort. Have we, in the schools, been equally sensitive to the probable effects on children of certain forms of rivalry and competition in our classrooms? Do we make great efforts to see to it that the conditions under which children will vie with each other are consistent with what we know about the life and growth of children? In the area of physical education many of these things have been considered, but in our actual daily practice in academic classrooms, are we lagging behind the culture? Are we insensitive to the need for feelings of trust and security?

6. *Are there some places where competition should be excluded?*

If we were to talk with leaders of American business and industry, we should soon come to know a number of situations in which they feel that competition has no place at all. They would feel that children should not have to compete for the love of their mother; this is based upon the assumption that there is enough love to go around the family and on the assumption that denying it to some might be devastating in its effects. Courtship relationships *before* marriage are often characterized by rivalry, but marriage is assumed to act as a block to unbridled competition for love. Extra-marital relationships are almost tabu in our culture. Do we have children competing for our love and attention in our classrooms or have we really communicated the idea that there is enough to go all the way around? Do we see a number of places where we do not want competition to be the motivation? If we don't, we are not in step with the culture as it has developed. We need to strive for relationships that promote trust and security.

7. *What about unfair, unethical practices?*
Where the goals focus on beating the other fellow; where prizes or grades are focused on pleasing teachers or parents; the issue may come to be so important that the participants will cheat, steal, and do many other things in order to get the coveted prize. These departures from good sportsmanship are evident in our culture (including industry) and in our schools. Those who engage in these sharp, shrewd, anything-to-win methods debase themselves as well as others in the human family. Punishing the behavior does little if any good. Helping children to understand what they are doing and why they are doing it may well be the first thing to do; a second would be to clarify the real purposes of being in school and how best these could be accomplished, and whether or not cooperativeness might be a better method of achieving feelings of trust and security.

8. *What about guarantees of security?*
Most of us are aware that many farmers are paid NOT to plant certain crops. These farmers have argued that they would be deprived of certain incomes if they did not plant those products, and they want to be guaranteed against losses. For many years our government has given this assurance by way of subsidies. Similarly we have subsidized new enterprises, and sometimes for many years after they were started. The airplane industry is but one example. The oil industry is given certain tax advantages and these amount to a guarantee of security. In some of our wartime contracts the government has paid all costs plus a certain percentage. In this situation the manufacturer is guaranteed security. In our schools do we guarantee security for children? Are we lagging behind the culture? Could we reduce the stresses and anxieties that are associated with the compe-

tition for grades, for awards, for prizes? Could we put more emphasis upon trust and feelings of security?

9. *Should we always compete against the highest standard?*
On a number of occasions children are told that they should always "do their best." Always? Or nearly always? Is the teacher always, or nearly always, dressed her very best? What about manners? Always, or nearly always, the very best? What about the looks of her apartment or of her house? Is it always, or nearly always, at its very best? What about the classroom? What about many other things, in school and at home? As adults we have developed a sense of discrimination about the idea of excellence and its relationship to a particular situation and to time. On many occasions we do what the situation demands or needs, and we aren't persnickety about a large number of extras which might make our efforts "our very best." At that time and in that situation we are pretty sure that we have met the requirements well. Shouldn't we be helping children to see when "the very best" is indeed needed, and when that standard can, and at times should, be relaxed? Shouldn't we be reducing stress and strain and deep anxieties? Isn't it part of our job to help children to feel more secure in the presence of alternatives?

10. *Is the schedule more important than anything else?*
Where children have very few choices of what they shall do during the day, their resentment is against the system. They have to compete against the program, and in a situation involving little choice, the children tend to lose. Where they have the feeling that the schedule is fixed in a deep rut, that each day is like the previous, and in each and every period of the day they "must" do what the schedule calls for, they cannot have much of a sense of security. The whole day and all of its periods constitute a veiled threat to their need for some freedom to choose, some feeling of relaxation, some periods wholly controlled by themselves.

11. *Are children people?*
Do we who are responsible for the growth and development of children think of them as real people? Or do we think of them as units of a kind which we manipulate to achieve *our* purposes? Most of us have tried to reduce the stresses in our own lives, and we have tried to modify the influence of competition in our own drives. We have joined organizations to protect our interests against strong and sometimes unethical adversaries. Children do not have such organization. It is our professional task to protect them from unusual and unfair competition of many kinds. Children represent a *captive* audi-

ence in our schools. By law, they have to be there. Should we take advantage of the situation by forcing unnecessary competition upon them? Should we see our task in ways that make them less secure? Or are they people too, and should our task be one of keeping up with the culture pattern? If we are to be in step with the present times, we need to make our schools less competitive, more cooperative, more concerned with the quality of life that every child is experiencing in our classrooms.

Having said all of this, I hasten to add as a summary note that competition isn't all bad. We can have fun and games that are competitive and at the same time not vicious and not dangerous to ongoing friendly relations among all the competitors. We can help children anticipate the possibilities of losing and how they would feel if and when they lose. We can talk about winning and losing and the conditions which make competition reasonably fair. We can, in the process, help our children see that the process needs to be rigorously controlled in terms of trust and security.

9

SOME
CONCLUDING
REMARKS

From experience I know that when authors write a book about calculus, the whole book from cover to cover focuses on calculus. I have wondered sometimes if anything other than calculus was at all important to those authors. As I re-read what I have written about the security feelings of children, I get a somewhat analogous impression. Has too great an emphasis been placed upon the idea of security out of relationship to the lives of children? I do hope that my frequent use of phrases which include the word *security* have not muted my concerns for the total, integral growth and development of boys and girls.

On several occasions I have indicated the high importance that I attach to the physical health of every child. I have stated very clearly that I am deeply concerned that this generation of children shall be given many opportunities to think for themselves. I have also emphasized the great importance of helping children to develop values and have made reference to a companion volume by this same publisher which deals only with the topic of values and teaching.[1]

---

[1] Louis E. Raths, Merrill Harmin, and Sidney B. Simon, *Values and Teaching* (Columbus: Charles E. Merrill Publishing Company, 1966).

In this present volume I have paid some attention to the idea of competition in the lives of children. I have written at length about power and morale in small face-to-face groups. I have given some attention to the ideas of people who do not agree with me on the great importance of the fulfillment of the eight emotional needs described at some length in these pages.

In all of this I have tried to bring home to the reader some of the feelings of children whose emotional needs are NOT being met. Suppose for a moment that you are a fifth grade teacher, and that in your room two boys have gotten into a furious fight with each other. Their fists are flying, there are tears to be seen, and there is even some bloodletting. Suppose also that some one should say to you: "Now would be a good time to teach those boys long division." Undoubtedly you would think this was an extremely stupid remark, and I would agree with you. What about those children who are "crying inside"? Some of them want love or praise or friends so very, very much, and they can only think about what they are lacking. They cannot hear us when we try to teach. Until we try to meet some of their needs, we shall probably be unsuccessful in our teaching efforts. And if we are able to satisfy some of these needs, just think of what a difference it will make in the life of the child. For him, the whole world will probably become a different place, a happier, more secure, more trusting and trustworthy place.

In these closing pages I want to say again that it is your professional job to help children to grow, to learn, to mature. The meeting of needs is not your sole responsibility. But, if unmet needs are getting in the way of a child's growth and development, his learning and his maturing, I insist that it is your obligation *to try* to meet his needs. I say that with conviction. I believe it from the bottom of my heart. And so do you, probably. I'm pretty sure that if a child needed glasses you would take some steps to help meet that need. And if a child had some difficulty in hearing you might make many efforts to help him to learn. And so also with unmet emotional needs.

Children cannot check their emotions at the door and we should not expect them to. We should be very much concerned about their feelings. I hope this book will help you to observe children in a new way, that it will help you to listen for clues to unmet needs, that it will have encouraged you to try out a whole range of these ideas with one or two children, and I hope the consequences will prove to be good.

I have also suggested a child's need to make choices. I have indicated my concerns for a richer curriculum, one that provides for individual differences, and one that gives all children chances to succeed and to have feelings of achievement.

It has often been said that we live only once, that we don't have a second or a third round. I wish that we could impress more fathers and mothers, more college teachers of education, more teachers generally, and more administrators, that all of us have *only one childhood* to live, and for many of us it is terribly grim and unhappy. Our children need more freedom, more choices, more dedicated concern from intelligent and compassionate adults. They need adults who are concerned about their needs, values, status, thinking, and who are trying to help us whenever we needed help.

I hope that all of us will begin to value children more than we ever did before, and I hope that this increased concern of ours will show up in this present generation of children. We can demonstrate, as it has never been demonstrated before, how happy the life of a child can be. What do you think? Will we do it?

BIBLIOGRAPHY

Alexander, Franz. *Psychosomatic Medicine.* New York: W. W. Norton & Co., 1950.

Ardrey, Robert. *The Territorial Imperative.* New York: Atheneum Publishers, 1966.

Bronfenbrenner, Urie. *Two Worlds of Childhood: U.S. and U.S.S.R.* With the assistance of John C. Condry. New York: Russell Sage Foundation, 1970.

Dollard, John, et al. *Frustration and Aggression.* New Haven: Yale University Press, 1939.

Dunbar, Helen Flanders. *Mind and Body.* New enl. ed. New York: Random House, 1955.

Frank, Lawrence Kelso. *The Fundamental Needs of the Child: A Guide for the Rearing and Education of Young Children.* New York: National Association for Mental Health, 1952.

———. *Nature and Human Nature: Man's Image of Himself.* Brunswick, N.J.: Rutgers University Press, 1951.

———. *Society as the Patient.* New York: Kennikat Press, 1948.

Halleday, James Lorimer. *Psychosocial Medicine.* New York: W. W. Norton & Co., 1948.

Lorenz, Konrad. *On Aggression.* New York: Harcourt, Brace & World, 1966.

Milbank Memorial Fund. *The Biology of Mental Health and Disease.* New York: Hoeber, 1952.

Mumford, Lewis. *The Conduct of Life.* Harcourt, Brace & Co., 1951.

Murray, Henry Alexander. *Explorations in Personality.* New York: Oxford University Press, 1938.

Plant, James Stuart. *The Envelope: A Study of the Impact of the World upon the Child.* New York: Commonwealth Fund, 1950.

Rajpal, P. L. "Improving the Preparation of Classroom Teachers." *College Student Journal,* in press.

Raths, Louis E.; Harmin, Merrill; and Simon, Sidney B. *Values and Teaching.* Columbus, Ohio: Charles E. Merrill Publishing Co., 1966.

Raths, Louis E.; Wassermann, Selma; Jonas, Arthur; and Rothstein, Arnold M. *Teaching for Thinking: Theory and Application.* Columbus, Ohio: Charles E. Merrill Publishing Co., 1967.

Ribble, Margaretha Antoinette. *The Rights of Infants: Early Psychological Needs and Their Satisfaction.* New York: Columbia University Press, 1943.

Saul, Leon Joseph. *The Hostile Mind.* New York: Random House, 1956.

INDEX